Gifts

FROM YOUR KITCHEN

Gifts

FROM YOUR KITCHEN

MAKE AND GIFT WRAP FABULOUS, HOME-MADE PRESENTS

Deborah Nicholas

SPRING HILL

Published by Spring Hill, an imprint of How To Books Ltd.
Spring Hill House, Spring Hill Road
Begbroke, Oxford OX5 1RX
United Kingdom
Tel: (01865) 375794
Fax: (01865) 379162
info@howtobooks.co.uk
www.howtobooks.co.uk

First published 2012

How To Books greatly reduce the carbon footprint of their books
by sourcing their typesetting and printing in the UK.

British Library Cataloguing in Publication Data
A catalogue record of this book is available from the British Library.

ISBN: 978 1 905862 99 3

Produced for How To Books by Deer Park Productions, Tavistock, Devon
Designed and typeset by Mousemat Design Ltd
Printed and bound by in Great Britain by Bell & Bain Ltd, Glasgow

Contents

Acknowledgements

I know I truly inherited my love of baking from my mum and for that I will always be grateful. None of this would have been possible without your help and encouragement all the way. Love you, mum!

I have been completely overwhelmed by the support I have received whilst putting together this book. Family and friends have helped with sourcing products and supplying me with decorative pretties for the photography. My ever-helpful husband has been my chauffer to and from the shops to stock up on a lifetime supply of icing sugar and flour! And my little helpers – Benjamin, Scott, Jacob, Ethan and Evangeline – gave me their ever-truthful critique of new recipes and what they would love to see (… I have spared you some of the truly unique ideas they had!)

Thank you so much to Nikki Reed and Spring Hill books for taking this chance on me, for being ever patient with my questions and for helping me through every step!

This is a dream come true for me and I hope you enjoy each and every gift within this book. The main thing to remember is have fun – I know I have!

Introduction

For as long as I can remember, my mum always baked. Birthdays and celebrations involved days of prep work and a house that smelled of cake and treats! Homemade scones and Victoria sponge cakes were a staple when it came to what we offered guests, and even today mum is still asked to bake for family occasions. Taking the time to show me how to cream butter and sugar together by hand until it reaches the right consistency, not yelling at me for trying to melt chocolate by pouring boiling water over it (I was 8 and it was my first solo attempt at crispy cakes!) and sitting with me in front of the oven gauging times and temperatures whilst I tried and tested new recipes for this book. I am so grateful that I inherited such a love of baking and all the support that has gone with it over the years.

When I was little, we would all sit and wait for the baking to cool before being allowed to try just one … these days I am lucky if I have the cookies out of the oven before the family are wrestling each other out of the way for first try! The joys of having a large family is that I can bake one day and it is all gone the next, which is a good thing when you have the baking bug and it comes to trying out new recipes! With 4 growing sons, I have to admit to finding it hard to fill them, which is why a lot of these recipes will make more than 24 treats. Cookies will keep in an airtight container for up to 5 days – if they last that long!

In this book, I will show you how to create simple handmade gifts, from cookies to fudge and facemasks to lip scrub! Whether you are a baker or simply aim for the handmade aspect of gift giving, everything contained within this book can be made from scratch and given from the heart!

For me, the presentation of gifts is a whole delight in itself! From picking which pretty patterned card to make the boxes from or whether to use silk or cotton ribbons, a small swing tag or completely over-the-top embellishment-adorned luggage tag … the choice is entirely yours to enjoy. Stack the cookies high in a window box and fasten with colour co-ordinated ribbons to match the chocolate chips or create white chocolate cookies and place them in a simple white box with a satin ribbon for the sophisticated look that you would pay a premium for in the shops.

I truly believe that each gift given should mean something, both to the creator and the recipient. Anyone can buy a cd or a movie but it means something special when you take the time to create a batch of cupcakes. Take this one step further and tailor make embellishments to adorn each one – theme them to the recipient's likes: if it's a little girl's birthday why not create a princess theme and make the strawberry and marshmallow cupcakes topped with sparkling pink sugar crystals. Pop them into a cupcake window box styled with ribbons and bows, lace and gems for a gift any true princess would treasure!

Within this book you will find treats and gifts for every occasion, follow these simple rules and you will not go wrong!

- Eggs are all large unless otherwise stated.
- Butter is at room temperature.
- I use a mixer to speed things up and take out the hard work so the instructions tell you what speed to use for mixing. If you are mixing by hand, you may need to mix for a little longer than recommended.
- Temperatures and baking times are guidelines only. Learn how your oven works and adapt times/temperatures to suit. Always keep a timer handy; it is so easy to get distracted and leave things longer than necessary!
- If possible, always bake straight onto baking sheets that have been sprayed with a little 1-calorie oil. I find this so much simpler than rubbing each tray with butter and lining. The spray prevents sticking and allows for easy clean after each use.
- When making the macaroons, please use parchment paper; the shells will stick to greaseproof paper as they are allowed to cool. You don't want to waste all that work!
- Always allow the baked goods to cool for 5 minutes on the baking trays before removing to cool completely on wire racks. This allows for the shape to be maintained and stops the food from cooling too quickly.
- Stored in airtight containers, cookies and cakes will last longer than normal: between 5 and 7 days. If you use fresh cream for the fillings or topping, remember to store them in the refrigerator and use within 2 days.
- Pickled goods will strengthen in flavour the longer they are left unopened. Ensure the jars and lids are fully sterilised before filling with hot liquid. Allow to cool before placing the lids on tightly and storing in a cool dark place.

I have enjoyed every minute of putting this book together. I hope you will have as much fun making unique gifts for your family and friends.

Debbie

1
Biscuits & Cookies

Store-bought cookies are so last season! If you want to impress and treat your guests to a little something special, then homemade biscuits are the way to go. Packed full of everything from fruit and nuts to chocolate and caramel, these sweet treats will become a gift-giving staple.

Apple & Sultana Cookies

MAKES 24

Including two of your five a day, these deliciously light cookies are a wonderful alternative to chocolate chips!

Ingredients

100g unsalted butter
100g light muscovado sugar
80g caster sugar
1 medium egg
1 tsp vanilla extract
100g plain flour
½ tsp bicarbonate of soda
½ tsp ground cinnamon
Pinch of salt
125g rolled oats
2 firm apples, peeled, cored and grated
80g sultanas

Method

1. Preheat the oven to 190°C/Gas 5. Grease and line 2 large baking trays.

2. Cream together the butter and sugars until fully combined.

3. Add the egg and the vanilla extract and beat lightly.

4. Sift in the flour, bicarbonate of soda, cinnamon and salt and mix on medium for 2 minutes.

5. Gently fold in the oats, grated apple and sultanas to ensure even distribution throughout the mix.

6. Place teaspoonfuls of the mix onto the baking trays, spaced 5cm apart to allow for spreading. You will need to bake in 2 batches or use 4 baking trays depending on your oven size.

7. Bake in the preheated oven for 12–15 minutes until lightly golden.

8. Remove from the oven and allow to cool for 5 minutes before transferring to wire racks to cool completely.

Giving as a Gift

Present this timeless classic in a hand-tied bouquet box. Lined with cotton and fastened with gingham ribbon, this would make the ideal gift for a vintage enthusiast!

How to make a tall window gift box, see page 164.

Apricot & Macadamia Nut Biscotti
MAKES 12

Biscotti are an adult indulgence. There is something so simple about being able to dip a biscuit in coffee that makes you feel like a continental grown up at the same time as feeling like a child!

Ingredients
135g granulated sugar
2 eggs
1 tsp vanilla extract
1 tsp baking powder
¼ tsp salt
245g plain flour
60g macadamia nuts, shelled and chopped
75g dried apricots, chopped into small pieces

Method

1. Preheat the oven to 180°C/Gas 4 and line a baking sheet with greaseproof paper.

2. In a bowl, beat the sugar and eggs on a high speed until thick, pale and fluffy (about 5 minutes). When you raise the beaters from the mixture, the egg mix will fall slowly down in ribbons. At this point, beat in the vanilla extract.

3. In a separate bowl, add the baking powder, salt and flour.

4. Add to the egg mixture and mix until fully combined.

5. Fold in the macadamia nuts and apricots.

6. Empty the mix onto your prepared baking sheet and, with wet hands, mould into a 30x10cm rectangle.

7. Bake in the preheated oven for 25 minutes or until golden brown.

8. Remove from the oven and place on a cooling rack for 10 minutes or until cool enough to cut.

9. Cut 2cm wide slices on the diagonal and place back on a tray (cut-side down) in the oven for a further 10 minutes. Turn them over after 10 minutes to brown the other side.

10. Remove from the oven and allow to cool on a wire rack.

11. Store for up to 14 days in an airtight container or wrap in greaseproof paper or baking parchment.

Giving as a Gift

Dip the ends of the biscotti in chocolate and allow to set. Place 3 pieces of the dipped biscotti into a pretty coffee cup and wrap the entire present in cellophane. Fasten with curling ribbons and a pretty handmade tag.

How to make a gift tag, see page 151.

Banoffee Bites
MAKES 12

Bananas and caramel work so well together that it made sense to create a sneaky treat that is disguised as a cookie but feels like dessert. These little bites can be dressed with cream and toffee sauce and will have you begging for more!

Ingredients
150g plain flour
150g wholemeal flour
50g light muscovado sugar
125g butter
1 egg
50ml cold water
¼ tsp ground cinnamon
2 small bananas, mashed
5 tbsp tinned caramel sauce
A little icing sugar, to serve

Method

1. Preheat the oven to 180°C/Gas 4. Grease and line 2 baking trays.

2. Put the plain flour, wholemeal flour, sugar, butter and egg in a food processor or blender and mix to breadcrumbs.

3. Add the water a little at a time until the mix comes together as a dough.

4. Knead the dough on a lightly floured surface and roll until 5mm thick.

5. Using a circular cookie cutter, cut out 24 circles.

6. Mix together the cinnamon, bananas and caramel and place a teaspoonful in the centre of 12 circles.

7. Create a seal for the lid by moistening around the edge of each cookie with a little water.

8. Gently add the additional 12 rounds as lids and press together with a fork to create a seal.

9. Make a small knife cut in the top of each banoffee bite to prevent them from bursting.

10. Bake in the preheated oven for 20–25 minutes or until lightly brown and firm to touch.

11. Allow to cool on baking trays for 5 minutes before transferring to cooling racks.

12. Sprinkle with icing sugar and serve.

Giving as a Gift

Line up these delicious treats in a rectangular presentation box with co-ordinating wrap.

How to make a tall window gift box, see page 164.

Alternatives

Instead of banana and caramel filling, why not try a more traditional fig centre. Heat 200g dried figs in a heavy-based pan to soften, then add to a blender and break down to a pulp. This can then be used following the recipe as above.

Chocolate Chip Cookies
MAKES 24

These cookies are a family favourite and our go-to recipe in times of need! An easy recipe that can be used over again and made in minutes – nothing says 'get well soon' like homemade cookies and a glass of cold milk.

Ingredients
225g butter
175g caster sugar
175g soft brown sugar
1 tsp vanilla extract
2 eggs
350g plain flour
1 tsp bicarbonate of soda
1 tsp salt
350g dark chocolate, chopped

Method

1. Preheat the oven to 190°C/Gas 5. Grease 4 large baking trays.

2. Cream together the butter, sugar and vanilla extract until smooth.

3. Add the eggs one at a time, scraping the mix down from the sides of the bowl to ensure it is all incorporated.

4. Stir in the flour, bicarbonate of soda and salt.

5. Gently fold in the chopped chocolate pieces.

6. Grease a 30cm length of clingfilm and place the mix in the centre. Form into a sausage shape and wrap completely in the film. Refrigerate for 30 minutes.

7. Once the mix is holding its shape, use a sharp knife to cut 1cm slices and roll them into rounds with floured hands.

8. Place on the prepared baking trays and flatten slightly with a palette knife.

9. Bake in the preheated oven for 10 minutes or until slightly golden.

10. Leave on the baking trays to cool slightly before transferring to wire racks to finish cooling.

Giving as a Gift

These cookies look great wrapped in greaseproof paper and fastened with a gingham ribbon. Add a little swing tag with a personal message to complete a great gift. Or stack them up in one of the long window boxes to give that professional look.

How to make a tall window gift box, see page 164.

Cranberry & Pistachio Cookies
MAKES 24

The green of the pistachios looks great against the pop of red cranberry, add a drizzle of dark chocolate and you have an award-winning combination. Enough to win over any cookie lover!

Ingredients

200g soft brown sugar
125g butter, at room temperature
3 eggs
½ tsp vanilla extract
150g plain flour
50g cocoa powder
½ tsp baking powder
100g dried cranberries, chopped
75g pistachio nuts, chopped
100g chocolate chips

Method

1. Preheat the oven to 180°C/Gas 4. Grease and line 2 large baking trays.

2. Mix the butter and sugar together until soft and creamy.

3. Add one egg at a time, scraping the mix down from the sides of the bowl between each addition to ensure all the mixture is incorporated. Add the vanilla extract.

4. In a separate bowl, sieve together the flour, cocoa powder and baking powder. Add one-third at a time to the butter mixture, making sure each time that the ingredients are fully mixed.

5. Gently fold in the dried cranberries and pistachio nuts.

6. Lightly flour your work surface with plain flour and carefully roll out the cookie mixture until approximately 5mm thick.

7. Cut out 24 cookies with a decorative cookie cutter and place on the prepared baking trays. Bake in the preheated oven for 12–15 minutes.

8. Remove from the oven and allow to cool on the baking trays for 5 minutes before transferring to wire racks to cool fully.

9. Melt the chocolate chips in a bowl above a pan of boiling water. Ensure the bowl does not touch the water.

10. Using a metal spoon, drizzle the melted chocolate over the now cooled cookies and allow to set before packaging.

11. Can be stored in an airtight container for up to 7 days.

Giving as a Gift

These cookies look exquisite packaged in the long window box and fastened with a dark cranberry silk ribbon.

How to make a tall window gift box, see page 164.

Stack the cookies on top of each other and wrap in cellophane before adding to a personalised gift pouch.

A simple homemade tag and floral embellishment give this special treat the finishing touch.

Cranberry & White Chocolate Cookies
MAKES 24

These cookies are perfect at Christmas when there is an abundance of fresh cranberries in the supermarkets but they can be made all year round with dried berries of any variety.

Ingredients
120g butter, softened
110g light brown sugar
100g caster sugar
2 tsp vanilla extract
1 egg
180g plain flour
1 tsp bicarbonate of soda
125g dried cranberries
140g white chocolate chips

Method

1. Preheat the oven to 190°C/Gas 5. Grease 4 large baking trays.

2. Cream together the butter, sugar and vanilla extract until smooth.

3. Add the egg, scraping the mix down from the sides of the bowl to ensure it is all incorporated.

4. Stir in the flour and bicarbonate of soda. Gently fold in the cranberries and chocolate chips.

5. Using your hands, create golf ball-size rounds.

6. Place onto the prepared baking trays and flatten slightly with a palette knife.

7. Bake in the preheated oven for 10 minutes or until slightly golden.

8. Leave on the baking trays to cool slightly before transferring to wire cooling racks.

Giving as a Gift

These cookies look great wrapped in greaseproof paper and fastened with a gingham ribbon. Add a little swing tag with a personal message to complete a great gift.

How to make a gift tag, see page 151.

Create a gift in a jar by layering the dry mix into a sterilised airtight jar.

Decorated Sugar Cookies
MAKES 24

These flooded cookies can be made in any shape and size. Theme to the recipient or event, and flood with royal icing or top with rolled fondant for a special finish.

Ingredients
240g caster sugar
120g butter
1 egg
1 tsp vanilla extract
350g plain flour
2 tsp baking powder
100g icing sugar
2 tbsp cold water
Colouring of your choice

Method

1. Preheat the oven to 180°C/Gas 4. Grease 3 large baking trays.

2. Cream together the sugar and butter.

3. Add the egg and vanilla extract and continue to mix.

4. Gradually add the sieved flour and the baking powder and mix until a firm ball is formed. You may need to take it out of an electric mixer to finish this step.

5. Roll it out onto a floured surface and use cookie cutters to cut your desired shapes.

6. Place them on the prepared baking trays and bake in the preheated oven for 15 minutes.

7. Remove from the oven and allow to cool on the baking trays before moving to cooling racks.

8. Once cooled completely, make up your icing to a hard peak consistency by mixing together the icing sugar and water. Pipe a border around the edges of each cookie.

9. Divide the remaining icing into separate dishes and colour as you wish.

10. Gradually add a few drops of water at a time until you end up with a thick, syrup-like liquid. Decant this into a squeezy bottle (available from kitchen or baking shops) and fill in each of the sections – this is called 'flooding'.

11. If necessary, use the tip of the bottle to push the icing gently if necessary towards the edge so it fills all the gaps.

12. Leave to harden.

Giving as a Gift

Pop the biscuits into a tin or canister, add a pretty homemade label and some ribbon and you have an inexpensive but very effective gift.

When tailoring to a party or special event, why not make a selection of different shapes. Bottles, booties, dummies and ducks work well for baby showers and would look great in the Tiffany-style box. Line with tissue paper and wrap with 'It's a boy/girl' ribbon for a gift that will be loved!

How to make a cupcake window box, see page 158.

Diva Shortbread
MAKES 24

A little piece of indulgence! Containing one of our favourite tipples and dusted with gold leaf, this shortbread is worthy of being served to any diva!

Ingredients

For the base:
175g unsalted butter
225g plain flour
100g caster sugar

For the filling and topping:
175g butter
175g caster sugar
3 tbsp golden syrup
400g can of condensed milk
2 tsp coffee cream liqueur
200g dark chocolate

Method

1. Preheat the oven to 180°C/Gas 4. Grease and line a 23x23cm square cake tin.

2. Place the butter, flour and sugar in a food processor and process until it starts to bind together. (This can be done by hand if preferred.)

3. Pour into the prepared baking tin and press with a metal spoon or palette knife to create a flat base.

4. Bake in the preheated oven for 20–25 minutes or until golden brown.

5. While the base is cooking, place the butter, sugar, syrup and condensed milk in a heavy-based pan.

6. Heat gently until the sugar has melted. Bring to the boil, reduce the heat and simmer for 6–8 minutes, stirring all the time, until very thick. Pour over the shortbread and chill in the refrigerator for 2 hours or until firm.

7. Place the chocolate pieces and cream liqueur in a bowl over a pan of boiling water and melt the chocolate gently ensuring the bowl does not come in contact with the water.

8. Allow to cool a little before spreading over the caramel. Use a fork to create a pattern on the top of the wet chocolate and allow to set for 1 hour in the refrigerator.

9. Gently dust with gold leaf for a diva-worthy dessert.

Giving as a Gift

Packaged in a glassine bag with bag topper or stacked in the rectangle window box with decorative ribbons, this shortbread will impress for any occasion.

How to make a tall window gift box, see page 164.

How to make a custom bag topper, see page 152.

Fig & Caramel Bites
MAKES 24

A grown-up version of the classic fig roll. With the addition of caramel, these sweet treats will have you walking down nostalgia lane with a whole new spring in your step!

Ingredients
250g self-raising flour
125g butter, at room temperature
Pinch of salt
2 tsp cold water to bind
125g dried figs
3 tbsp tinned caramel sauce
2 tbsp double cream

Method

1. Preheat the oven to 180°C/Gas 4. Using a spray oil, lightly spray a 24-hole patty tin.

2. In a medium bowl, rub together the flour, butter and salt with your fingertips until light breadcrumbs are formed.

3. Add a little water at a time until the mix is bound together.

4. Lightly flour the work surface and roll out the pastry until 5mm thick.

5. Cut out small rounds with a cookie cutter and, using your fingers, lightly press the pastry into the patty tins.

6. Place the figs, caramel sauce and cream in a heavy-based pan and heat gently until the resulting filling is soft to touch.

7. Spoon a small amount into each of the pastry cases and bake in the preheated oven for 15–20 minutes.

8. Remove from the oven and allow to cool in the tray for 5 minutes before transferring to a wire rack to cool completely.

9. The bites can be served hot or cold.

Giving as a Gift

The decorative sleeve on the wrap around box makes this treat seem like a blast from the past. Packaging that takes you back in time is almost as important as the filling itself – I said almost!

How to make a self-fastening gift box, see page 175.

Mixed Nut Party Cookies

MAKES 24

These nut-filled cookies have a surprise in every bite! Baked as a lollipop, they can be presented as a deliciously different alternative to cake pops.

Ingredients

125g butter, at room temperature

125g dark muscovado sugar

1 egg, beaten

1 tsp vanilla extract

180g self-raising flour

2 tbsp cocoa powder

100g dark chocolate chips

85g mixed nuts, chopped

Method

1. Preheat the oven to 190°/Gas 5. Grease 2 large baking trays.

2. Add butter and sugar to a bowl and cream until fluffy.

3. Gradually beat in the eggs and vanilla extract, scraping the mix down from the sides to ensure it is fully incorporated.

4. Sift the flour and cocoa and add to the mix. Gently fold in the chocolate chips and nuts.

5. Drop large walnut-sized balls of mix onto the baking trays, leaving plenty of space to allow for spreading during cooking. Press the lollipop sticks into the mixture and mould the cookie mix lightly to form a seal around the sticks.

6. Bake in the preheated oven for 12–15 minutes or until golden brown.

7. Remove from the oven and allow to cool slightly before transferring to wire racks to cool completely.

Giving as a Gift

Wrap the lollies in cellophane and ribbons and present in the desk tidy box.

How to make a coffee treats box, see page 180.

Alternatives

These would be ideal as a party surprise. Bake the cookies without pressing them into a cookie shape – leave as walnut-size balls and insert the sticks so that it stands vertical. Cook as above and allow to cool completely. Melt a bowl of chocolate and dip the lollies so that they are completely covered. No one will guess they are cookies until they bite into the nutty centre!

Sour Cherry & Pistachio Cookies

MAKES 24

Sweet and simple biscuits to impress, even on short notice. You can whip these up in an hour so no more biscuit-less cups of coffee!

Ingredients

75g icing sugar

225g soft butter

1 tsp vanilla extract

225g plain flour

100g chocolate

50g pistachios, chopped

50g sour cherries, chopped

Method

1. Preheat the oven to 170°C/Gas 4. Grease and line 2 large baking trays.

2. Cream together the icing sugar and butter until light and fluffy.

3. Add the vanilla extract and sift the flour into the butter mix. Using a spatula make sure all of the mix is loosened from the sides of the bowl.

4. Tip onto greased clingfilm and mould into a round.

5. Place in the refrigerator to harden slightly for approximately 30 minutes.

6. Remove from the fridge and roll out on a lightly floured surface.

7. Cut out the required shapes and lay them on the prepared trays.

8. Bake in the preheated oven for 15–18 minutes.

9. Remove from the oven and leave to cool on wire racks.

10. Melt the chocolate in a heatproof bowl over a pan of boiling water.

11. Using a small spoon, pool a little of the chocolate on top of each cookie.

12. Sprinkle with the chopped pistachios and sour cherries.

13. Drizzle with the remaining melted chocolate and allow to set completely before transferring to an airtight tin.

Giving as a Gift

These cookies can be topped with anything you prefer! For a summer gift, why not add dried strawberries and coconut before topping with the chocolate. Layer them side by side in the window treat box or stack together in a pillow pouch!

How to make a tall window gift box, see page 164.

How to make a pillow pouch, see page 156.

Stained Glass Rounds
MAKES 24

There is something about stained glass windows that make everyone smile. You can now create your own little works of art by baking boiled sweets into shortbread!

Ingredients
125g butter
55g caster sugar
180g plain flour
1 egg yolk
24 coloured boiled sweets

Method

1. Preheat the oven to 190°C/Gas 5. Grease and line 3 large baking trays.

2. In a medium bowl, beat together the butter and sugar until light and creamy.

3. Add the flour and egg yolk and mix together until fully combined.

4. Empty onto a floured surface and roll out to 1cm thick.

5. Using a shaped cookie cutter, cut out your shapes and place on the baking trays. Use a smaller cookie cutter to take out the centre of each biscuit.

6. Pop one of the boiled sweets into the open centre of each biscuit and bake in the preheated oven for 15–20 minutes. Remove from the oven when the biscuits are lightly golden and the boiled sweets fully melted.

7. Allow to cool completely on the trays before removing and packaging. This will allow the clear centre to harden completely.

Giving as a Gift

These shortbreads are ideal to use as Christmas decorations on the tree! Cut a little hole into the biscuit before baking, which is where you can thread ribbon to hang. When the light catches the clear coloured centre, it will give a stained glass sparkle! Package in a handmade double-ended box or stack in a tower and fasten with ribbons.

How to make a double-ended gift box, see page 182.

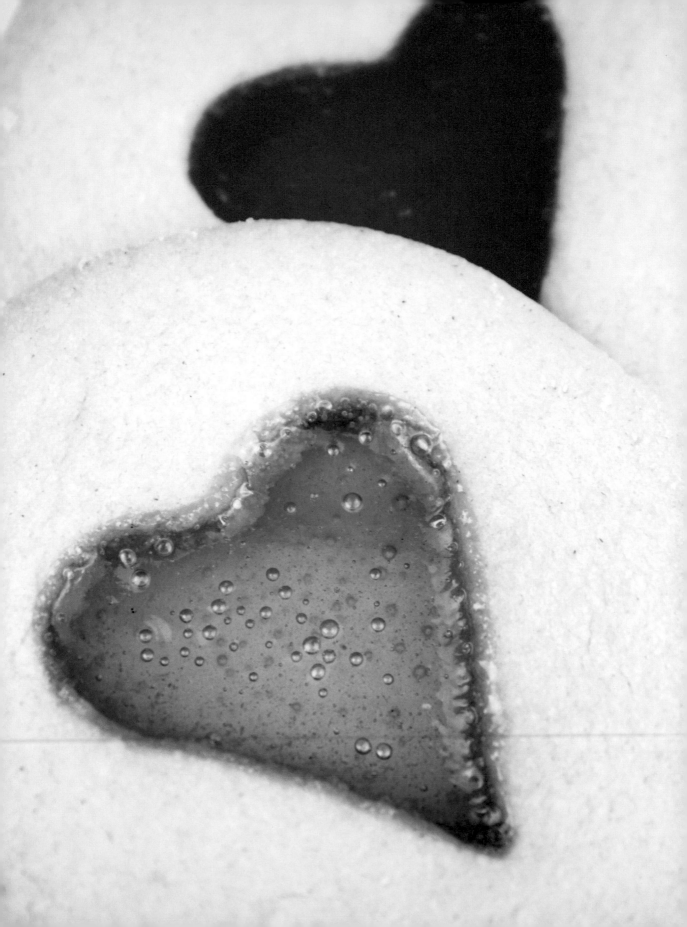

Stem Ginger Rosettes
MAKES 24

These kept me sane while I was pregnant! The crunchy outer hides a soft and decadent centre – the tang of ginger against the sweet vanilla base makes these cookies delicious.

Ingredients

125g butter, at room temperature
200g caster sugar
2 tsp vanilla extract
1 egg
2 tbsp black treacle
300g plain flour
1 tsp bicarbonate of soda
¾ tsp ground cinnamon
½ tsp ground cloves
¼ tsp salt
1 tbsp ground ginger
1cm length fresh stem ginger, finely chopped

Method

1. Preheat the oven to 180°C/Gas 4. Grease and line 4 large baking trays.

2. Cream together the butter, sugar and vanilla extract until smooth.

3. Add the egg and black treacle. Scrape the mix down from the sides of the bowl to ensure it is all incorporated.

4. Stir in the flour, bicarbonate of soda, cinnamon, cloves, salt and ground ginger.

5. Gently fold in the chopped stem ginger.

6. Add the mix to a large heavyweight piping bag fitted with a large star nozzle. Pipe 24 rosettes onto the prepared baking trays.

7. Bake in the preheated oven for 10–12 minutes or until golden.

8. Leave on the baking trays to cool slightly before transferring to wire cooling racks.

Giving as a Gift

Line a small gift basket with greaseproof paper and layer with the ginger rosettes. Wrap with cellophane and finish with a length of pretty ribbon and gift tag. The perfect gift for pregnant ladies!

Instead of piping into rosettes, roll the mixture to a 5mm thick round and cut into hearts with cookie cutters. Cut a small rectangle out of the bottom of the heart and bake as directed above.

Dip the cooled fingers into melted dark chocolate for a more decadent cookie which can then be hooked onto the side of a china cup.

Present these in the coffee treats box.

How to make a coffee treats box, see page 180.

2
Cakes

Nothing impresses more than a single cupcake flourished with a mountain of frosting and decorative sprinkles! Whether you prefer tray bakes, single serving cakes or mountainous layers of sponge, each one of the following will be a cake lover's idea of heaven!

Banana, Walnut & Honey Loaf
MAKES 1 X 2LB LOAF OR 6 MINI LOAVES

Don't throw out those over-ripe bananas! The sweetened, soft texture makes a great base for this loaf. The addition of walnuts and honey make it the ideal treat for those cold winter mornings when you need a little pick-me-up.

Ingredients
125g butter
60g caster sugar
300g bananas, mashed
75g walnuts, finely chopped
2 tsp pure honey
175g plain flour
1 tsp bicarbonate of soda
Pinch of salt

Method

1. Preheat the oven to 180°C/Gas 4. Grease and flour 2 x 2lb or 12 mini loaf tins.

2. In a medium bowl, cream together the butter and sugar until light and fluffy.

3. Add the bananas, walnuts and honey and combine on a slow speed for 2 minutes.

4. In a separate bowl, sieve together the flour, bicarbonate of soda and salt.

5. A little at a time, add the flour mix to the butter mix, working together for a further 2 minutes.

6. Empty the mixture into the prepared tin(s) and bake in the preheated oven for 40–45 minutes for the large loaf or 25–30 minutes for the mini loaves.

7. Remove from the oven and allow to cool slightly in the tins before transferring to a wire rack to cool completely.

8. Store in an airtight container for up to 7 days.

Giving as a Gift

Homemade loaves are probably among the best presents to receive, as everyone loves how they look. Freshly baked and wrapped in cellophane fastened with ribbons, this delicious present will give off a wonderful aroma when unwrapped!

After baking the banana loaf in the mini tins, allow to cool completely and transfer back to the baking tins for presentation. Place inside one of the tied gift boxes and present to a baker for the perfect treat!

Banoffee Muffins
MAKES 12

Banoffee pie is one of our favourite family desserts – what could be better than bananas covered in toffee, cream and chocolate? These individual banoffee muffins are a rich, filling and quick substitute, meaning you get an individual dessert for a fraction of the time and effort.

Ingredients

For the cake:
75g butter
150g caster sugar
1 large egg
3 large bananas
200g plain flour
1 tsp bicarbonate of soda
½ tsp baking powder
½ tsp salt
400g tinned caramel sauce

For the topping:
300g icing sugar
50g butter, softened
50g mascarpone cheese
100g fudge, chopped

Method

1. Preheat the oven to 180°C/Gas 4. Line a baking tray with 12 large muffin or cupcake cases.

2. Mix the butter and sugar together in a mixing bowl until fully combined.

3. Add the egg, scraping the mix down from the sides of the bowl if needed.

4. Next, mash the bananas onto a plate to make sure there are no big lumps. This is ready now to be added to the sugar and butter mix. Beat together slowly for about 1 minute.

5. In a separate bowl, sift together the flour, bicarbonate of soda, baking powder and salt. Add the sieved flour to the mixing bowl containing the rest of the ingredients and leave on medium speed for about 4 minutes or until smooth.

6. Bake in the centre of the preheated oven for 15 minutes. Remove when a cake skewer inserted into the centre of the cake comes out clean. Leave in the tray for 5 minutes to hold their shape before moving to a cooling rack to cool completely.

7. Once the cakes are completely cooled, scoop out the centre and add a spoonful of the caramel. Place the removed piece of cake on top of the caramel to create a seal.

8. To make the frosting, add the icing sugar and butter to a mixer and, using the paddle tool if you have one, blend together until soft and firm. Add the mascarpone cheese, blending until smooth and light.

9. Using a large nozzle piping bag, pipe the icing onto the top of the cakes and sprinkle with the diced fudge pieces.

Giving as a Gift

These treats look fabulous in a specially designed cupcake window box – the recipient can get a sneak preview of what is in store for them! Use pretty coloured card chosen specially for the recipient. Fasten with ribbons and add a little gift tag for a perfect picnic dessert.

How to make a cupcake window box, see page 158.

Alternatives

Heat a little of the caramel sauce and use it to drizzle across the top of a freshly whipped cream topping for a decadent summer treat!

Why not make a toffee flavour frosting by adding some of the caramel to the frosting mix – start with 1 tbsp, then add more as required. Finish with a dried banana chip or chocolate chips for those with a sweet tooth!

Black Forest Whoopie Pies
MAKES 24

These soft and fluffy, double-bite desserts are so simple it's almost sinful! Chocolate sponge drops are sandwiched together with a tangy cranberry jelly, sweet fresh creamed cheese and a sharp bite of freeze-dried fruit.

Ingredients

For the pies:
- 100g unsalted butter
- 175g muscovado sugar
- 1 egg
- 300g plain flour
- 35g cocoa powder
- 1 tsp bicarbonate of soda
- 1 tsp baking powder
- Pinch of salt
- 1 tsp vanilla extract
- 125ml semi-skimmed milk

For the filling:
- 50g butter, softened
- 300g icing sugar, plus more for dusting
- 50g soft cream cheese
- 50g freeze-dried winter fruits
- Cranberry jam

Method

1. Preheat the oven to 180°C/Gas 4. Grease and line 6 baking sheets.

2. Mix together the butter, sugar and egg until well blended and creamy.

3. Sieve together the flour, cocoa, bicarbonate of soda, baking powder and salt into a separate bowl.

4. Stir the vanilla extract and milk together in a small bowl.

5. Add spoonfuls of the milk mixture and the flour mixture alternately to the creamed butter and sugar until fully incorporated and a smooth silky mix is formed.

6. Load the silky mixture into a large piping bag with a plain round nozzle. Pipe into small rounds onto the prepared baking sheets.

7. Bake in the preheated oven for 15 minutes until the whoopie pies have a slight give when pressed.

8. Leave to cool completely on a wire rack.

9. To make the filling, cream together the butter and icing sugar until smooth. Add the cream cheese and continue to beat with an electric hand mixer until fully incorporated and stiff peaks are formed.

10. Gently fold in the dried fruits. Put the filling mixture into a large piping bag with a plain large nozzle, ready to pipe the filling into the whoopie pies.

11. Take 2 of the cooled sponge halves and spread one with the cranberry jam. The other should be piped with a large helping of the forest fruits cream. Sandwich both together before dusting with icing sugar to serve.

12. Store in an airtight container and eat within 4 days.

Giving as a Gift

These treats look fabulous in a window box – the recipient can get a sneak preview of what's in store for them! Fasten with ribbons and add a little gift tag for a perfect picnic dessert.

How to create the tall window gift box, see page 164.

How about providing these as 'ready to make' gifts? Give the whoopie sponge cakes alongside a little jar of homemade jam and pot of the home-infused cream filling. These will keep unmade, in airtight conditions, for up to 7 days.

Choose your favourite sponge flavour and combine with all sorts of delicious fillings to create your own mouthwatering presents.

Alternatives

Instead of chocolate whoopie pies, just leave out the cocoa powder to create vanilla versions, adding the equivalent weight of flour. Fill these with lemon curd and fresh cream.

Substitute desiccated coconut for the cocoa powder and add a tablespoon of Malibu to the cream mix for a delicious Caribbean-style adult treat!

Fill with whipped cream and jam and serve with tea as a delicate alternative to Victoria sponge for Gran's birthday or cover with melted chocolate and sprinkles for a little one's tea party – the choices are endless!

Cherry & Almond Cupcakes
MAKES 12

A soft, light cake, with a rich, dark, cherry filling and topped with sweet frosting and crunchy almonds – a combination of everything your sweet tooth could ever wish for!

Ingredients

For the cakes:
120g plain flour
140g caster sugar
1½ tsp baking powder
40g butter
120ml whole milk
¼ tsp vanilla extract
1 egg

For the filling and frosting:
12 tbsp Morello cherry jam
200g sugar
80ml water
¼ tsp cream of tartar
1 tsp vanilla extract
2 egg whites
50g flaked almonds

Method

1. Preheat the oven to 180°C/Gas 4. Prepare a muffin tin with 12 cases.

2. In a large bowl, cream together the flour, sugar, baking powder and butter. Add half the milk and continue to blend together.

3. In a separate bowl, add the vanilla extract to the remaining milk and beat together lightly.

4. Add the milk mix to the large bowl and blend until fully combined.

5. Using an ice-cream scoop, place a spoonful in each cupcake case and bake for 15–18 minutes or until a cake skewer, inserted in the centre of the cake, comes out clean.

6. Remove from the oven and allow to cool in the tin for 5 minutes before moving to a wire rack to cool completely.

7. Once cooled, scoop out the centre of each cake and fill with a tbsp of Morello cherry jam. Replace the removed cake as a lid for the jam filling.

8. To make the frosting, add the sugar, water and cream of tartar to a heavy-based pan.

9. Cook over medium-high heat until the sugar is dissolved and the mixture is bubbly.

10. In a medium mixing bowl, whisk the egg whites and vanilla to soft peaks.

11. Gradually add the sugar mixture while whipping constantly until stiff peaks form, about 7–10 minutes.

12. Decant into a large piping bag with large star-shaped nozzle and pipe onto the cupcakes.

13. Whilst the topping is still sticky, sprinkle with the flaked almonds.

Giving as a Gift

Display the cakes in a pretty box and tie with a matching ribbon.

How to make a cupcake window box, see page 158.

Alternatives

Alternatively place all the dry ingredients into a glass jar and fasten with a label detailing how the recipient can make the cupcakes themselves!

Christmas Muffins
MAKES 12

When you have a husband who could live on sweet mince pies alone, you know you have to take action! These muffins were created out of sheer desperation in wanting to have something lighter than pastry day in day out. I am sure you will be baking these all year round and remember – a muffin is for life, not just Christmas!

Ingredients
150g caster sugar
75g butter, at room temperature
80ml milk
1 egg
200g plain flour
1 tsp bicarbonate of soda
½ tsp baking powder
1 banana
125g sweet mincemeat
Ground cinnamon
12 whole glacé cherries

Method

1. Preheat the oven to 180°C/Gas 4. Line a 12-cup cupcake tray with decorative cases and set aside.

2. In a medium bowl, mix together the sugar, butter, milk and egg.

3. Sieve in the flour, bicarbonate of soda and baking powder while continuing to mix.

4. Crush the banana with the back of a fork. Gently fold the banana and sweet mincemeat into the mixture and spoon into the prepared baking cases.

5. Sprinkle with cinnamon and place a glacé cherry in the centre of each case before placing in the preheated oven for 15–18 minutes.

6. Remove from the oven when a cake skewer inserted into the centre of the cake comes out clean.

7. Allow to stand for 5 minutes before transferring to a wire rack to cool fully.

Giving as a Gift

Impress your friends by enclosing the cupcakes in a handmade cupcake gift box. With the addition of the transparent window, this cute box makes the perfect presentation idea.

How to make a cupcake window box, page 158.

Alternatively place all the dry ingredients into a jar and present as a ready-to-make gift. All the recipient needs to do is add the wet ingredients. The addition of a handwritten label explaining the process and what needs to be added makes this a perfect DIY gift for those new to baking.

Alternatives

Eaten as it is, this makes a delightful breakfast muffin. However, it can be easily turned into a sweet treat with the simple addition of cinnamon frosting.

Create the cream cheese frosting on page 40 with $\frac{1}{2}$ tsp ground cinnamon added at the mixing stage. Spoon the mix into a piping bag fitted with a large star nozzle and use to top the muffins.

The cakes will keep for up to 5 days in an airtight container.

Coconut & Lime Cake
SERVES 12

The soft coconut and tart lime of this cake work well together, making a mouth-watering combination suitable for afternoon tea or elevensies. You can make this in a 30cm square cake tin or 2 x 20cm round tins

Ingredients

For the cake:
200g butter
4 eggs
200g self-raising flour
1 tsp baking powder
100g desiccated coconut
2 tsp Malibu

For the frosting:
200g caster sugar
½ tsp cream of tartar
80ml water
Grated zest and juice of 1 lime
1 tsp Malibu
3 egg whites
100g desiccated coconut

Method

1. Preheat the oven to 180°C/Gas 4. Grease and line 1 x 30cm square baking tin or 2 x 20cm round baking tins.

2. Cream together the butter and sugar. Add the eggs one at a time, scraping the mix down from the sides between each addition.

3. In a separate bowl, add the baking power to the flour and spoon into the butter mix until fully incorporated.

4. Stir in the desiccated coconut and add the Malibu, folding in gently.

5. Decant into the prepared square baking tin or divide between 2 round cake tins and smooth the surface.

6. Bake in the preheated oven for 25 minutes.

7. While the cake is cooling, make up the frosting. Put the sugar, cream of tartar, water, Malibu and lime juice and zest together in a pan and heat until clear and bubbling.

8. Allow to cool slightly, then pour into a mixer or bowl and add the egg whites. Whisk on high speed for 10 minutes.

9. While waiting for the frosting to cool completely, toast the coconut in a heavy-based pan until lightly browned. Be careful not to let it catch the bottom of the pan – it literally takes 2 minutes to brown.

10. Remove cake from oven and allow to cool slightly before transferring to a wire rack to cool fully.

11. If you have made the 2 round cakes, they need sandwiching together. Place one of your cakes top-down on a cake stand or plate, to create a flat platform for the frosting.

12. Add about one-third of the frosting and level out with a palette knife to create a smooth surface for the second layer. Add the second cake.

13. Cover the complete outside of the cake, top and sides, in the frosting mix. If you have made one cake, simply cover the top and sides with frosting.

14. Sprinkle the finished cake with toasted coconut.

Giving as a Gift

The frosting will not store well as it deteriorates quickly so decorate just before giving as a gift. This cake is best presented on a vintage tea plate, wrapped with cellophane and fastened with lace. Alternatively you could make up the cakes and prepare the ingredients for the frosting in a jar like the marshmallow frosting (see page 58).

Coconut & Pineapple Cupcakes
MAKES 12

A taste of the tropics! These cakes can be made with or without the Malibu so can be shared with the children – of course that's a matter of choice!

Ingredients

For the cakes:
120g plain flour
140g caster sugar
1½ tsp baking powder
40g butter
120ml whole milk
¼ tsp vanilla extract
1 egg
4 pineapple rings, finely chopped
2 tsp Malibu

For the frosting:
200g caster sugar
1 tsp Malibu
½ tsp cream of tartar
80ml water
3 egg whites
100g shredded coconut

Method

1. Preheat the oven to 180°C/Gas 4. Prepare a muffin tin with 12 cases.

2. In a large bowl, cream together the flour, sugar, baking powder and butter. Add half the milk and continue to blend together.

3. In a separate bowl, add the vanilla extract to the remaining milk and the egg and beat together lightly.

4. Add the milk mix to the large bowl and mix until fully combined.

5. Gently fold in the pineapple pieces and Malibu.

6. Using an ice-cream scoop, place a spoonful of the mixture in each cupcake case and bake in the preheated oven for 15–18 minutes or until a cake skewer, removed from the centre of the cake, comes out clean.

7. Remove from the oven and allow to cool in the tin for 5 minutes before moving to a wire rack to cool completely.

8. While the cake is cooling, make up the frosting. Mix the sugar, Malibu, cream of tartar and water together in a pan and heat until clear and bubbling.

9. Allow to cool slightly, then pour into a mixer or bowl and add the egg whites. Whisk on high speed for 10 minutes.

10. Once the frosting is completely cool, fill a large piping bag and fit with a large star nozzle.

11. Pipe swirls to the top of each cake and top with the coconut.

Giving as a Gift

The cupcake window box is the ideal packaging for these delicious cakes. Fastened with a citrus-coloured ribbon, a cocktail umbrella and a recipe for a non-alcoholic cocktail, this gift will be loved by any recipient.

How to make a cupcake window box, see page 158.

Hidden Surprise Cupcakes
MAKES 12

Sometimes you deserve more than just a cake ... sometimes you deserve a cake with biscuit baked into the centre! Go on, spoil yourself and surprise those around you by having your cake and biscuit and eating them both at the same time!

Ingredients

For the cake:
125g soft margarine
175g caster sugar
2 eggs
1 tsp vanilla extract
175g self-raising flour
1 tsp baking powder
12 large Oreo cookies

For the frosting:
300g icing sugar
50g butter, softened
50g mascarpone
  cheese
1 vanilla pod, split
12 mini Oreo cookies

Method

1. Preheat the oven to 180°C/Gas 4. Line a 12-hole muffin tin with paper cases.

2. In a medium size bowl, cream together the butter and sugar. Add the eggs one at a time, scraping the mix down from the sides of the bowl between additions.

3. Add the vanilla extract and mix well.

4. In a separate bowl sieve together the flour and baking powder. Spoon the flour into the butter mix and combine fully before spooning into the 12 cupcake cases.

5. Press 1 Oreo cookie down into the centre of each case so the cake mix covers the cookie completely.

6. Bake in the preheated oven for 18–22 minutes until golden brown. A cake skewer, inserted into the centre, should come out clean.

7. Remove from the oven and allow to cool in the tray for 5 minutes before transferring to a wire rack to cool completely before decorating.

8. To make the frosting, combine the icing sugar and butter in a mixer on medium speed.

9. Add the mascarpone cheese. Scrape the seeds from the vanilla pod into the mix and blend on high until soft and fluffy.

10. Decant the frosting into a piping bag fitted with a large star nozzle and pipe onto the top of each cake. Finish with a mini Oreo as decoration.

Giving as a Gift

The purpose-built cupcake boxes work as an ideal display and packaging solution for the decorated cupcakes. The cupcakes are held securely in place and can then be transported and presented in perfect condition.

How to make a cupcake window box, see page 158.

Mountainous Rocky Road
SERVES 24

This is my add-everything version of Nigella Lawson's Christmas rocky road! The combination of different textures, flavours and colours makes this a die-hard favourite for children and grown ups – one piece is never enough!

Ingredients

175g dark chocolate

175g milk chocolate

175g butter

4 tbsp golden syrup

200g Lebkuchen biscuits (German gingerbread biscuits)

50g white chocolate chips

100g brazil nuts

50g pecan nuts

100g whole dark cherries

50g whole apricots, halved

125g mini marshmallows

Icing sugar, for dusting

Method

1. Prepare a 30cm high-sided baking tin with greaseproof paper.

2. Melt the dark chocolate, milk chocolate, butter and golden syrup together in a bowl over a pan of boiling water. Do not let the bowl touch the water.

3. Remove from the heat and allow to cool slightly.

4. Break the Lebkuchen biscuits into rough bite-size pieces. Chop some of the nuts in half and leave some whole for extra bite.

5. Add all the remaining ingredients except the icing sugar to the bowl of warm chocolate and stir until everything is completely coated.

6. Empty the contents of the bowl into the prepared tin and allow to cool completely before cutting into squares and serving dusted with icing sugar.

Giving as a Gift

The small window box will fit one piece of this delicious gift, or alternatively if you can give away more, add 3 pieces to the hand-tied gift box.

Layer the dry ingredients in a glass bowl. Wrap the bowl in a decorative tea towel and fasten with ribbon. A simple note giving directions on how to make this decadent treat is a rewarding gift for any kitchen lover.

How to make the a cupcake window box, see page 158.

How to make a hand-tied gift box, see page 173.

Raspberry & White Chocolate Mini Loaves
MAKES 12

The soft, tart raspberries with the creamy white chocolate make for a delightful contrast in these individual mini loaves.

Ingredients

300g caster sugar

225g butter

300g self-raising flour

2 tsp baking powder

4 eggs

50ml milk

200g fresh raspberries, halved

150g white chocolate, finely chopped

Method

1. Preheat the oven to 180°C/Gas 4. Grease 12 individual mini loaf tins.

2. In a large bowl, add the caster sugar, butter, self-raising flour, baking powder, eggs and milk. Mix together until smooth and silky.

3. Add the raspberries and white chocolate. Fold in gently with a spatula until fully combined. Do not overwork, as this will break down the chocolate and raspberries.

4. Half fill the mini loaf tins and bake in the preheated oven for 20–25 minutes.

5. Remove from the oven and allow to cool before transferring to wire rack to cool completely.

Giving as a Gift

Wrap in greaseproof paper and tie with string for that rustic, shabby chic look.

If you are making the muffins, present in the cupcake boxes for a professional hand-baked gift.

How to make a cupcake window box, see page 158.

Alternatives

Why not make these into muffins. Make them in exactly the same way, pop the mixture into muffin cases instead of loaf tins and bake for 20–25 minutes at 180°C/Gas 4.

To create a topping for the muffins, place 300ml whipping cream, 100g icing sugar and 150g fresh raspberries into a mixer and beat on high until light and fluffy. Pipe on to the top of the muffins and sprinkle with grated white chocolate.

S'more Bars
MAKES 16–18

This treat was inspired by the American tradition of toasting s'mores around a campfire. Campers layer Graham crackers, chocolate and marshmallows and toast them until hot and gooey! This variation is delicious hot or cold and holds together well for up to 3 days.

Ingredients
125g unsalted butter, melted
50g caster sugar
225g digestive biscuits, crushed
5 tbsp smooth peanut butter
400g milk chocolate
150g mini marshmallows

Method

1. Place the butter, sugar and crushed biscuits into a pan and heat through until all the butter is soaked into the biscuit mix.

2. Remove from heat and stir in the peanut butter.

3. Press into a greased 20cm square tin and chill for 20 minutes.

4. Put the chocolate in a bowl and place over a pan of boiling water to melt. Make sure the bowl does not touch the water.

5. Remove the base from the fridge and carefully pour over the chocolate until fully covered.

6. Place back in the refrigerator until the chocolate has set.

7. Sprinkle with the mini marshmallows to create a level topping. Do not add too many marshmallows as it will burn before the lower ones have a chance to warm through.

8. Place under a preheated grill for 3-4 minutes until gold and bubbly.

9. Wait until cooled before cutting into pieces and serving.

Giving as a Gift

An ideal picnic treat, this looks wonderful given wrapped in greaseproof paper and string. Fasten a little swing tag saying, 'I love you s'more'. Pop into a clear glassine bag, embellish with a bag topper and fasten with ribbon.

How to make a custom bag topper, see page 152.

Strawberry & Marshmallow Cupcakes
MAKES 12

Plain vanilla cupcakes with a gooey strawberry centre, topped with a light and fluffy marshmallow frosting. A sure fire winner to give to anyone with a sweet tooth!

Ingredients

For the cakes:
120g plain flour
140g caster sugar
1½ tsp baking powder
40g butter
120ml whole milk
1 egg
¼ tsp vanilla extract

For the filling and frosting:
12 tbsp strawberry jam
200g sugar
80ml water
¼ tsp cream of tartar
2 egg whites
1 tsp vanilla extract
3 tbsp dried strawberry chips
75g mini marshmallows, chopped

Method

1. Preheat the oven to 180°C/Gas 4. Line a muffin tin with 12 paper cases.

2. In a large bowl, cream together the flour, sugar, baking powder and butter. Add half of the milk and continue to blend together.

3. In a separate bowl, add the vanilla extract to the egg and the remaining milk and beat together lightly.

4. Add the milk mix to the large bowl and mix until fully combined.

5. Using an ice-cream scoop, place a spoonful of the mixture in each cupcake case and bake for 15–18 minutes or until a cake skewer, removed from the centre of the cake, comes out clean.

6. Remove from the oven and allow to cool in the tin for 5 minutes before moving to a wire rack to cool completely.

7. Once cooled, scoop out the centre of each cake and fill with 1 tbsp of strawberry jam. Replace the removed cake as a lid for the jam filling.

8. To make the frosting, add the sugar, water and cream of tartar to a heavy-based pan. Cook over medium-high heat until the sugar is dissolved and the mixture is bubbly.

9. In a medium mixing bowl, whisk the egg whites and vanilla to soft peaks.

10. Gradually add the sugar mixture while whisking constantly until stiff peaks form, about 7–10 minutes.

11. Allow to cool completely before stirring in the dried strawberry chips.

12. Decant into a large piping bag with large star-shaped nozzle and pipe onto the cupcakes.

13. Whilst the topping is still sticky, sprinkle with the cut marshmallows.

Giving as a Gift

How to make a cupcake window box, see page 158.

Alternatively create one of the paper baskets, line with doilies and stack with fresh strawberries. Place the cupcakes within the fresh fruit for a delicious way to get your five a day!

Tangy Lemon Cake
SERVES 8

Sometimes it is the simple recipes that have the most impact, and this tangy lemon cake couldn't be easier!

Ingredients
125g soft margarine
180g caster sugar
180g self-raising flour
1 tsp baking powder
2 eggs
4 tbsp milk
Grated zest of 1 lemon
A little icing sugar, for sprinkling

Method

1. Preheat the oven to 180°C/Gas 4. Grease and line an 18cm round cake tin.

2. Add all of the ingredients to a mixing bowl and either mix by hand or machine for 2 minutes until fully incorporated and silky smooth.

3. Empty into the prepared tin and level the top with a wooden spoon.

4. Bake in the preheated oven for 35–40 minutes or until a cake skewer, inserted into the centre, comes out clean.

5. Allow to cool for 10 minutes in the tin before turning out onto a wire cake rack to cool fully.

6. Sprinkle with icing sugar before serving.

Giving as a Gift

This cake is such an easy gift to make and can be baked in small loaf tins or individual baking cases.

Allow to cool, dust with icing sugar and wrap in cellophane, fastening with a decorative ribbon and handwritten tag.

Alternatives

Add 50g caster sugar to the juice of 1 lemon and pour over the cake while still warm. The lemon will sink into the sponge and the sugar will crystalise, forming a crunchy topping on the outside of the cake.

Alternatively make a lemon icing to drizzle over the cake once it has cooled completely. Mix 120g icing sugar with 5 tbsp lemon juice until you get a runny consistency, pour over the cake and allow to set before serving.

Toffee & Pecan Cupcakes
MAKES 12

A true comfort cupcake. The soft caramel toffee and sweet pecan chunks combine to make a deliciously addictive treat! Adapted from the Primrose Bakery plain vanilla cupcakes, these simple additions make a world of difference.

Ingredients

For the cakes:
120g plain flour
140g caster sugar
1½ tsp baking powder
40g butter
120ml whole milk
1 egg
¼ tsp vanilla extract
100g pecans, finely chopped
3 tbsp caramel sauce

For the topping:
250g icing sugar
80g butter
3 tbsp caramel sauce

Method

1. Preheat the oven to 180°C/Gas 4. Line a muffin tin with 12 paper cases.

2. In a large bowl, cream together the flour, sugar, baking powder and butter. Add half the milk and continue to blend together.

3. In a separate bowl, add the vanilla extract to the egg and the remaining milk and beat together lightly.

4. Add the milk mix to the large bowl and mix until fully combined.

5. Gently fold in 50g of the chopped pecans and the caramel sauce.

6. Using an ice-cream scoop, place a spoonful in each cupcake case and bake in the preheated even for 18–20 minutes or until a cake skewer, removed from the centre of the cake, comes out clean.

7. Remove from the oven and allow to cool in the tin for 5 minutes before moving to a wire rack to cool completely.

8. To make the frosting, sieve the icing sugar into a bowl, add the butter and caramel sauce. Beat together until light and fluffy.

9. Using a palette knife, spread on the top of each cupcake to cover.

10. Spread the remaining 50g of chopped pecans onto a plate and dip the entire surface of the cupcakes in the nuts.

Giving as a Gift

Create a double cupcake box for a gift to share or create a single box for that special person.

Decorate with a handmade gift tag, paper roses and doily for a perfect treat to show you care – presentation is the key!

How to make a double-ended gift box, see page 182.

How to make a hand-tied gift box, see page 173.

Alternatives

All different kinds of nuts work well with toffee, from almonds to hazelnuts. Why not try toasting the pecan nuts in brown sugar first to get a caramelised finish.

Salted caramel is on everyone's lips right now – create your own by gently frying together 50g salted nuts with 20g of dark brown sugar.

3
Sweets

No gift is complete without sweets or chocolate. A lot of store-bought chocolates rely heavily on huge boxes or overstuffed packaging, which then only contain a small amount of that special treat. Homemade chocolates and fudge can be piled high for a fraction of the costs.

Candied Peel
MAKES 24

Use this colourful decoration as a simple and effective finishing touch, adding to cakes, ice-creams and desserts. Keep in a jar and use as needed.

Ingredients
200g orange peel sliced
200g grapefruit peel, sliced
200g lemon peel, sliced
100ml water
400g granulated sugar

Method

1. Line a large baking tray with baking parchment.

2. Put the orange, grapefruit, lemon peel and water in a heavy-based saucepan. Heat until boiling, then simmer for 10 minutes until the peel softens. Rinse and repeat.

3. In a separate pan, heat the granulated sugar over a low heat until just boiled. Add the peel and stir to coat in the syrup.

4. With a slotted spoon, remove the peel from liquid, place on the prepared baking tray and leave for about 2 hours to harden.

5. Place in an airtight jar and use as decorative topping to cakes, ice-creams and desserts.

Giving as a Gift

Using glass paint, create designs on plain jars to highlight the sweet sugary contents. Add a ribbon and swing tag with serving suggestions.

How to make a gift tag, see page 151.

Chocolate Slabs
MAKES 1 LARGE OR 5 SMALL SLABS

A simple creation which is a chocoholic dream! Bars of chocolate filled with all your favourite candies, fruits and nuts! You can use non-stick chocolate moulds, or line a loaf tin with baking parchment.

Ingredients

500g good-quality dark chocolate

300g your own favourite candies, dried fruits, mixed nuts

Method

1. Line a loaf tin with baking parchment, if using. Lightly oil your tins if they are not non-stick.

2. Melt the chocolate in a heatproof bowl over a pan of boiling water. Do not let the bowl touch the water.

3. Pour the melted chocolate into prepared moulds and allow to cool slightly.

4. Sprinkle your chosen toppings onto the chocolate and press down slightly to adhere.

5. Refrigerate until solid, then carefully remove from moulds.

Giving as a Gift

These chocolate slabs sell for a fortune in top chocolate stores, so make a lovely gift. Simply wrap the bar in cellophane and tie with ribbon and a tag.

Add one of the chocolate slabs to a clear gift bags and create a bag topper to explain what is contained within.

How to make a custom bag topper, see page 152.

When pouring, use circular moulds and present them as chocolate pizzas in the perfect handmade pizza boxes.

How to make a pizza box, see page 170.

Suggested toppings

Dried: cranberries, apricots, prunes, pineapple pieces, apple slices, raisins, banana chips.

Candies: chocolate straws, chocolate-coated peanuts, chocolate raisins, mini eggs, broken chocolate chunks, fizzy candies, strawberry laces, Smarties, jelly beans, Maltesers, chocolate coins, popping candy.

Nuts: Brazil, cashew, pistachio, walnut, hazelnut, pecan, chopped mixed nuts, salted peanuts, almonds.

Chocolate Truffles
MAKES 24

Truffles are probably the easiest yet most delightful chocolates to give as a gift. They portray an exquisite chocolatier working all day when really they are so quick and easy! Cover in an assortment of toppings to really get the mouth watering!

Ingredients
200g good-quality dark chocolate
2 tbsp Amaretto
50g butter
4 tbsp icing sugar
75g ground almonds
50g plain chocolate, grated, to decorate

Method

1. Place 24 sweet cases on a baking tray.

2. Place the chocolate and liqueur in a heatproof bowl and set over a pan of boiling water until melted. Do not allow the bowl to touch the water. Remove from the heat.

3. Add the butter to the bowl and stir until melted.

4. Stir in the icing sugar and ground almonds.

5. Leave to cool until firm enough to roll into balls.

6. Roll the balls into the grated chocolate and place in the tray of sweet cases.

7. Chill in the fridge until ready to serve.

Giving as a Gift

Any handmade box would be perfect for truffles: a little sneak glimpse through the clear window of the cupcake box, truffles stacked in the little tower of drawers or simply lined up in a hand-tied gift bag.

How to make a cupcake window box, see page 158.

How to make a chest of drawers, see page 177.

How to make a hand-tied gift box, see page 173.

Why not simply pop a few into a cellophane bag, then gather up and finish with vintage lace for that decadent feel.

Alternative toppings

Sugar crystals, chopped nuts, popping candy, chocolate curls, icing sugar, white chocolate, freeze-dried fruits and so much more. While the truffles are still moist, roll them in your preferred topping to ensure they stick perfectly.

Coconut Marshmallow
MAKES 24 SQUARES

This super-soft, easy-to-make marshmallow will have your sweet tooth begging for more!

Ingredients
35g powdered gelatine
350ml hot water
200g caster sugar
Desiccated coconut, to decorate

Method

1. In a large electric mixer bowl, add the powdered gelatine and pour over 100ml of the hot water. Stir to dissolve.

2. In a separate bowl, dissolve the caster sugar in the remaining water.

3. Pour the sugar water into the gelatine and turn the mixer to high speed for 5 minutes. (You can use a hand mixer if needed.)

4. As the mixture cools, it will start to set. Pour quickly into a 20cm square silicone baking tray.

5. Allow to set for 2 hours before turning out, cutting into squares and coating with the coconut.

6. Store in an airtight container for up to 1 week.

Giving as a Gift

The coconut will stop the marshmallows sticking together, pile them high in a paper basket, wrapped in cellophane and fastened with a swing tag and ribbons.

How to make a paper basket, see page 154.

To make marshmallow of different colours, divide the mixture at step 2 and colour half with a few drops of food colouring. Pour into 2 baking trays and allow to set. When finished, alternate coloured layers in the handmade cupcake box, so the window allows the recipient to have a little hint of the treat in store.

How to make a cupcake window box, see page 158.

Crystallised Rose Petals

A delicate touch to the most romantic of flowers! Use as edible decorations on cupcakes and desserts.

Ingredients
1 large organic, pesticide-free rose
1 egg white, lightly beaten
60g icing sugar

Method

1. Gently pull the petals from the rose.

2. Using a small, fine paintbrush, carefully brush each petal with the beaten egg white. Coat both sides.

3. Coat each petal with sifted icing sugar and lay on a large lined baking tray to harden.

Giving as a Gift

The delicate nature of the rose petals means that they cannot be presented in bags for fear of damage. Place them in an airtight jar and fasten with ribbon. A single live rose would make the perfect partner to this romantic gift.

Easy Chocolate Fudge
MAKES 60 PIECES

This is so easy to make and tastes divine – a flavour somewhere between fudge and ganache!

Ingredients

400g good-quality dark or milk chocolate, finely chopped
397g can condensed milk
25g butter
100g icing sugar
55g roasted chopped nuts (optional)

Method

1. Put the chocolate in a non-stick saucepan with the condensed milk and butter and heat very gently, stirring occasionally, until melted and smooth. (Alternatively place these ingredients into a microwave-safe bowl and microwave in 10–20 second bursts, stirring frequently until the mixture is silky smooth.)

2. Beat the icing sugar into the mixture until combined thoroughly.

3. Press the fudge into a 18cm square tin, smooth over the top and press the nuts into the surface, if using.

4. Chill in the fridge for 1 hour until set, then cut into small squares.

Giving as a Gift

Fill the handmade stacking drawers with this fudge or place in a sweet bag and hide inside one of the sweet treat pouches.

How to make a chest of drawers, see page 177.

How to make a sweet treat pouch, see page 166.

Alternatives

Try any nuts or dried fruit you like in this recipe – pecans, pistachios, walnuts, hazelnuts and almonds all work really well. Or you could try adding cranberries, blueberries or even mini marshmallows!
For Christmas fudge, look out for glittery decorations – silver balls or even silver or gold leaf for a really special present.

Fruit & Nut Buttons
MAKES 24

So simple and easy to make, yet so much more flavoursome than plain chocolate drops.

Ingredients

200g good-quality dark chocolate

150g freeze-dried fruits

100g chopped mixed nuts

Method

1. Place the chocolate in a heatproof bowl over a pan of boiling water. Do not allow the bowl to touch the water. Stir until melted.

2. Remove from heat and stir in half the freeze-dried fruit and three-quarters of the mixed nuts.

3. Stir until all the fruit and nuts are covered in chocolate and spoon into button or sweet moulds.

4. Whilst the chocolate is still wet, sprinkle the remaining fruit and nuts over the top of each button.

5. Allow to set completely before removing from the button tray.

Giving as a Gift

Drop a handful of the buttons into a gift bag and embellish with a bag topper.

Alternatively, create the gift basket, line with tissue paper and pile up the buttons, or stack in the mini drawers with fresh berries or whole nuts.

How to make a custom bag topper, see page 152.

How to make a paper gift basket, see page 154.

How to make a chest of drawers, see page 177.

Macaroons
MAKES 48

Deliciously light, melt-in-the-mouth little parcels of coloured joy! A treat for young and old – once mastered never forgotten!

Ingredients
For the macaroons:
125g icing sugar
125g ground almonds
3 large egg whites
2 tbsp cold water
110g caster sugar
Food colouring (optional)
For the filling:
150ml double cream, whipped

Method

1. Preheat the oven to 160°C/Gas 3. Line 2 large baking trays with baking paper.

2. Place the icing sugar, ground almonds and half the egg whites together in a large bowl and mix to a paste.

3. Put the water and caster sugar in a small pan and heat gently to melt the sugar.

4. Turn up the heat and boil until the mixture starts to thicken to a syrup.

5. Whisk the remaining egg whites in a small bowl until medium-stiff peaks form when the whisk is removed.

6. Pour the sugar syrup into the whisked egg whites, whisking until the mixture becomes stiff and shiny.

7. For coloured macaroons, add a few drops of food colouring.

8. Spoon this meringue mixture into the almond paste mixture and fold gently until the mix becomes shiny and stands to peaks once more.

9. Spoon into a large piping bag fitted with a large plain nozzle.

10. Pipe small circles onto the lined tray, about 2cm apart, twisting the bag to finish each one with a small peak – this will flatten and leave a smooth finish

11. Leave to stand for 30 minutes or until a skin forms on the macaroons and they are dry to the touch.

12. Bake in the preheated oven for 12–15 minutes.

13. Remove from the oven, lift the paper off the baking tray and leave the macaroons to cool on the paper.

14. When cool, sandwich the macaroons together with whipped cream.

15. Once filled, they will keep for up to 3 days in the refrigerator, but longer if you leave them without filling or sandwich them with ganache.

Giving as a Gift

Stacked in a gift box and presented with a mini tub of ganache and whipped cream, these macaroons would make a delicious gift for anyone!

Alternatively, sandwich together and present in the cupcake window box for a treat to be remembered!

How to make a Tiffany-style gift box, see page 168.

Alternatives

Colours and toppings can vary to taste on these macaroons – why not add a drop of blue food colouring and whip blueberries with the cream for a light summer dessert.

A small drop of red food colouring and popping candy in the filling would work great for children's parties.

If you prefer not to use colouring, why not tint the mix with fresh raspberry juice for pink or blueberry juice for blue. Kiwi juice gives a great green colour, whilst a tiny hint of turmeric will turn the mix yellow. As with everything, use in moderation so as not to taint the flavour.

Mini Rose Meringue Kisses
MAKES 48

Crunchy yet chewy, these little pink kisses can be eaten alone or sandwiched together with fresh cream or ganache.

Ingredients

4 egg whites

125g caster sugar

4 drops of pink food colouring

3 drops of rose water

1 tsp cream of tartar

Method

1. Preheat the oven to 110°C/Gas ¼. Line 3 large trays with baking paper.

2. In a large mixing bowl, add the egg white and whisk on medium speed until the mixture stands in peaks when the whisk is removed.

3. Turn the speed to high and add the sugar, a little at a time, until thick and glossy.

4. Add the colouring, rose water and cream of tartar. Whisk on high speed for 2 minutes until stiff peaks are formed when the whisk is lifted.

5. Using a spatula, place the mixture in a large piping bag with a large rosette nozzle.

6. Pipe onto the prepared trays and bake in the preheated oven for 1 hour.

7. Remove before the meringues brown and allow to cool slightly before moving to a wire rack to cool completely.

8. Store in an airtight container for up to 1 month.

Giving as a Gift

The hand-tied gift box would the perfect gift presentation for these little kisses. Parcelled with a small pot of homemade chocolate ganache and a miniature butter knife for application, this would make an ideal picnic gift or wedding favour.

To make hand-tied gift box, see page 173.

Peanut Brittle
MAKES ENOUGH TO COVER 30CM^2 (BEFORE BROKEN INTO PIECES)

Everyone knows Nigella Lawson is a goddess – simple as that! This is my personal variation inspired by her simple peanut brittle. The addition of honey and cinnamon makes this brittle very moreish and slightly addictive ... don't say I didn't warn you!

Ingredients
200g caster sugar
60ml water
2 tbsp strongly flavoured honey
150g golden syrup
150g salted peanuts
1½ tsp vanilla extract
1 tsp ground cinnamon
25g soft butter
1¼ tsp bicarbonate of soda

Method

1. Take out a large sheet of baking parchment and set it beside the stove ready to receive the brittle once it is ready to pour.

2. Add the sugar, water, honey and syrup to a pan and gently bring to the boil. Turn up the heat and let it boil seriously for 10 minutes. It will be smoking by then so be warned! (Stand over it all the time to make sure it does not catch – mine did the first time and the house smelled of burnt toffee for days!) Be very careful as the sugar will be seriously hot.

3. Take the pan off the heat and, with a wooden spoon, stir in the nuts, followed by the vanilla, cinnamon, butter and bicarbonate of soda. You will have a golden, frothy, hot and gooey mix.

4. Pour this quickly onto the waiting parchment and, using an oiled wooden spoon, coax and pull it to make a nut-studded sheet, puddle-shaped rather than heaped.

5. Leave it to cool, then break into pieces and store in an airtight container in the refrigerator. Eat within 14 days.

Giving as a Gift

Peanut brittle is best presented in either greaseproof bags or glass jars – you can buy glassine bags, which look fabulous with a printed label topper and ribbon fastening. Glass jars keep the air away from the brittle, allowing it to last a little longer. Print a cute 'From the kitchen of ...' label and fasten with a colourful ribbon for a simple homemade gift.

How to make a custom bag topper, see page 152.

Alternatives

If available, you could use corn syrup instead of golden syrup – it is becoming more popular in the UK and available to buy in more supermarkets. This will result in a darker, clearer-looking brittle whereas the golden syrup creates a more cloudy, golden effect.

Why not coat the hardened brittle pieces in chocolate? Simply melt some good-quality dark chocolate over a pan of boiling water (ensuring the bowl does not touch the water) and carefully dip each piece of brittle in the chocolate. Leave to harden on a cooling rack placed over a sheet of baking parchment so that any excess chocolate drips away (but you can eat the drips!)

Raspberry & Chocolate Mousse
SERVES 4

This delicious and light dessert can be prepared a day in advance. Save time by adding the coulis and fresh raspberries just before serving with a sprig of fresh mint and a little grating of dark chocolate.

Ingredients

For the raspberry mousse:
250g fresh raspberries
20g icing sugar, sifted
200ml double cream
For the chocolate mousse:
250g good-quality dark chocolate
25g butter
30ml Grand Marnier
4 eggs, separated
100ml double cream
¼ tsp cream of tartar
40g caster sugar

For the raspberry coulis:
200g fresh raspberries
50g icing sugar, sifted
1 tsp lemon juice
For the garnish and filling:
100g fresh raspberries
Grated chocolate

Method

1. To make the raspberry mousse, add the raspberries and icing sugar to a food processor and mix until well blended. Press through a sieve to create a purée.

2. Whisk the double cream until it forms soft peaks, then and gently fold in the raspberry purée. Refrigerate until needed.

3. To make the chocolate mousse, melt the chocolate and butter in a bowl over a pan of hot but not boiling water. Make sure the bowl does not touch the water.

4. Remove from the heat and whisk in the Grand Marnier.

5. Beat the egg yolks until smooth, then and beat into the warm chocolate.

6. In a separate bowl, whisk the cream until soft peaks are formed. Add a spoonful of cream to the chocolate mix and fold until combined. Transfer the chocolate to the bowl with the remainder of the cream and fold in gently.

7. Whisk the egg whites until frothy, add the cream of tartar and continue whisking just until soft peaks are formed. Do not over-whisk.

8. Fold in a half the egg whites to the chocolate mix with a metal spoon, then gently fold in the remaining egg whites.

9. To serve, spoon a layer of fresh raspberries in the bottom of the serving glasses. Spoon the chocolate mousse on top of the raspberries until the glass is a little over half full. Tap the glass to level before adding the layer of raspberry mousse. Chill in the refrigerator.

10. To make the coulis, add the raspberries, icing sugar and lemon juice to a food processor and blitz on high for 2 minutes. Press through a sieve to create a purée.

11. Spoon a layer of the raspberry coulis onto the mousse and chill before serving.

Giving as a Gift

Dessert containers with lids can be bought at specialist cake stores (see page 192). A small decorative spoon fastened to the container with pretty ribbon would make a picnic that little bit more special.

Tipsy Fruit
MAKES 24

A decadent treat for adults only!

Ingredients
300g dried mixed apricots and prunes
100ml flavoured clear liqueur
200g good-quality dark chocolate
Icing sugar, for dusting
500g almond paste
50g white chocolate

Method

1. Put the fruits and liqueur in an airtight jar and allow to infuse overnight.

2. Place a sheet of greaseproof paper over a baking sheet.

3. Melt the dark chocolate in a bowl over a pan of hot water, making sure the bowl does not touch the water. Melt fully, then remove from the heat and allow to cool slightly.

4. On a surface that has been lightly dusted with icing sugar, roll out the almond paste to 5mm thick.

5. Use an 8cm circular cookie cutter to cut 24 rounds of marzipan.

6. Place one of the soaked fruits in the centre of each round and gently pull up the marzipan to cover the fruit entirely.

7. Drop each marzipan-wrapped fruit into the bowl of melted chocolate and turn to coat completely. Use a fork to remove from the chocolate and place on the greaseproof paper until the chocolate has set.

8. Melt the white chocolate as you did earlier for the dark chocolate.

9. Place the marzipan fruits onto wire racks and drizzle the white chocolate lightly over the top to create patterns on the top of each treat.

Giving as a Gift

Present these treats in an adorable handmade basket.

Pile 7 fruits together in the centre of a large circle of cellophane. Pull up and gather the cellophane, then fasten with sheer gold ribbon for an ideal Christmas treat.

Store in an airtight container for up to 2 weeks.

How to make a paper basket, see page 154.

Turkish Delight
MAKES 40 PIECES

Turkish Delight was originally a royal dish, exclusively made and served to royalty but fortunately we are now all allowed to enjoy it. It can contain an assortment of fruit and nuts but the mainstream flavours are rose and lemon.

Ingredients
100g cornflour, plus extra for sprinkling
450g granulated sugar
½ tsp lemon juice
630ml cold water
½ tsp cream of tartar
1 tbsp rose water
A few drops of food colouring (optional)
100g icing sugar

Method

1. Lightly grease a 20cm square baking tin and sprinkle with cornflour.

2. Place the sugar, lemon juice and 150ml of the water in a heavy-based saucepan over a medium heat. Stir until the sugar has dissolved and the mixture starts to boil.

3. Reduce the heat and simmer, without stirring, until the mixture reaches the soft-ball stage, 114–118°C, or when you can drip a drop of the mixture into cold water and mould it into a ball that will flatten when squashed but still retain its shape. Remove from the heat.

4. In a separate large, heavy-based saucepan over a low heat, stir together 75g of the cornflour with the cream of tartar. Gradually add the remaining water, stirring constantly so no lumps form. Stir until the mixture boils and creates a thick paste.

5. Carefully pour the hot sugar syrup into the paste and stir constantly. Reduce the heat and simmer for 1 hour, stirring frequently to prevent sticking.

6. Stir in the rose water and drops of food colouring, if using.

7. Pour the mixture into the prepared baking tin and smooth the surface. Leave overnight to set.

8. Sift the icing sugar and remaining cornflour onto a large cutting board and, using a sharp, oiled knife, cut the Turkish Delight into 2cm squares.

9. Allow all sides of the Turkish Delight to dry out for at least 2 hours to prevent sticking.

10. Roll each piece in the icing sugar mix to coat well.

11. Store in an airtight container, alternating layers of Turkish Delight with icing sugar and waxed paper to prevent the pieces sticking together.

Giving as a Gift

Traditional store-bought Turkish Delight is usually presented in a hexagonal box, lined with tissue paper and mountains of icing sugar. The cupcake window box is perfect to show your friend the treats in store.

How to make a cupcake window box, see page 158.

4
Bags

Whether paper, tissue, clear glassine gift bags or simple food bags, this is by far the easiest way to give gifts. Airtight bags are perfect for keeping gifts fresh for longer.

You can tie with ribbon to make them extra special and tie on a personal gift tag. You'll find some tips and templates on page 151.

Cheese Straws
MAKES 24

Why make life harder than it needs to be? When you are in a hurry, one of the best inventions is ready-roll pastry! You could make your own pastry but if you are in need of a savoury treat in a hurry then this is ideal recipe for you.

Ingredients

1 x 375g packet ready-rolled puff pastry
Flour, for dusting
50g unsalted butter, melted
4 tbsp sundried tomato paste
5 tbsp grated Parmesan cheese
2 tbsp chopped flat leaf parsley
1 egg yolk, beaten

Method

1. Preheat the oven to 210°C/Gas 7. Grease 2 large baking trays.

2. Lightly flour the work surface and roll the pastry to create an even square. Trim the edges as needed so that all the straws cook uniformly.

3. Brush the pastry with the melted butter.

4. On the top half of the pastry, spread the tomato paste and sprinkle with 4 tbsp of the Parmesan cheese and the parsley.

5. Fold the bottom half over the top half and press down lightly.

6. Brush the pastry with beaten egg yolk and sprinkle with the remaining Parmesan cheese.

7. With a large sharp knife, cut the pastry lengthways into 1cm strips.

8. Hold each end and carefully twist in opposite directions.

9. Place the strips onto the prepared baking trays, spacing evenly apart to allow space to puff.

10. Bake in the preheated oven for 10–12 minutes or until crisp and golden brown.

11. Allow to cool slightly on the trays before transferring to wire racks to cool completely.

Giving as a Gift

Create one of the sweet treat pouches and stand 6 cheese straws inside, fasten the pouch tight with ribbon to help the gift stand alone.

Why not present these cheese straws in a gift box with a jar of homemade spicy tomato chutney.

How to make the Spicy Tomato Chutney, see page 110.

How to make the sweet treat pouch, see page 166.

DIY Hot Chocolate
SERVES 2

Nothing warms a cold night like delicious, thick hot chocolate! This gift makes 2 large mugs of thick, creamy chocolate topped with mini marshmallows!

Ingredients

8 tbsp hot chocolate drink mix

100g dark chocolate chips

75g mini marshmallows

Method

1. Place the hot chocolate drink mix into the bottom of a cone-shaped candy bag.

2. Top with the dark chocolate chips.

3. Add the final layer of marshmallows and fasten with ribbon to seal.

Giving as a Gift

Add a swing tag with directions on how to make up the gift. For example:

Add the hot chocolate powder and chocolate chips to a mug and pour in 200ml of boiling water. Stir until the chocolate chips have melted, then and top with the marshmallows. Drink and enjoy. xxx

How to make a gift tag, see page 151.

Herbal Teas
MAKES 16 ASSORTED GIFT SACHETS

There are a wild variety of herbs and fruit infusions on the market. Just add to hot water to make a delicious and refreshing drink.

Ingredients

For the infusions:
4 cinnamon sticks
8 dried apple slices
Grated zest of 2 lemons
4 x 1cm pieces of
   stem ginger
4 sprigs of mint
4 x 1 cm pieces
   of liquorice root
12 dried banana chips
40g dried sour cherries
1 vanilla pod, quartered

Also required:
2 x 6cm squares of
   muslin
Thread and needle
Un-dyed string

Method

1. To make each gift sachet, sew 2 x 6cm squares of muslin together, leaving one of the sides open to add the ingredients.

2. In each of the first 4 sachets, place 1 crushed stick of cinnamon and 2 slices of the dried apple.

3. The next 4 sachets should contain the grated zest of half a lemon and 1 piece of stem ginger.

4. Strip the leaves from the sprigs of mint and add those along with a piece of liquorice root to the next 4 sachets.

5. The final 4 sachets will each contain 3 banana chips, 10g of sour cherries and a quarter of the vanilla pod.

6. Sew the final side of each sachet so that the ingredients are completely sealed inside. Stitch in place a length of un-dyed string and add a little tab at the end explaining which flavour infusion is enclosed.

Giving as a Gift

Stand the sachets alongside each other in one of the window boxes or present in a self-fastening box just as they would be sold in stores.

How to make a cupcake window box, see page 158.

How to make a self-fastening gift box, see page 175.

Mulled Wine Spice Bag

Fasten to a bottle of red wine for that ultimate Christmas gift, a spicy treat that perks up even the coldest of nights.

Ingredients
1 cinnamon stick
20 whole cloves
2 tsp mixed peel
2 cardamom pods
5 whole allspice
Also required:
20cm square of muslin

Method

1. Place all of the ingredients into the centre of the muslin square and bring up two opposite corners.

2. Fasten into a knot and repeat for the remaining corners.

3. Bring the ends of the first knot over the second knot and tie again to prevent any knots from slipping.

Giving as a Gift

Add a swing tag with ingredients and instructions and fasten to neck of a red wine bottle. Do not use died ribbon or string as the colours will transfer when boiled in the wine!

How to make a swing tag, see page 151.

Parmesan & Rosemary Crackers
MAKES 24

This recipe is for delicious savoury crackers which work well alone, as a snack, or with cheeses and chutneys.

Ingredients
180g plain flour
175g unsalted butter
200g Parmesan cheese, grated
2 tbsp rosemary
Flour, for dusting

Method

1. Preheat the oven to 180°C/Gas 4. Line 2 baking sheets with greaseproof paper.

2. Add the flour and butter to a large bowl and rub together.

3. Add the Parmesan and rosemary to the bowl and mould all the ingredients together to create a dough.

4. Wrap in clingfilm and place in the refrigerator for at least 1 hour.

5. Lightly flour the work surface and roll out the dough until 1 cm thick. Using a circular cookie cutter, cut out the 24 crackers and place on the prepared baking sheets.

6. Bake in the preheated oven for 12–15 minutes or until lightly golden.

7. Allow to cool for 5 minutes on the baking sheets before transferring to a wire rack.

Giving as a Gift

Present the biscuits piled high in the tall window gift box or pop a few into a cellophane gift bag, fasten with ribbon and place as little treats in lunch boxes.

How to make a tall window gift box, see page 164.

5
Jars

From granola to pickles, this section will show you how to create long-lasting gifts that will keep when stored. They can be made in advance, in bulk, to save any last-minute gift dilemmas.
A personal gift tag will make the gift special. You'll find some tips and templates on page 151.

Fruit & Nut Granola
MAKES 6 SERVINGS

Nothing starts a morning better than a bowl of homemade cereal. Top with natural yoghurt, milk or simply pop in a bag and munch on the way to work. This fruity, crunchy and downright moreish granola will help start your day with a smile!

Ingredients

200g rolled oats
100g dried apricots, finely chopped
100g walnuts, halved
100g dried cranberries, halved
50g flaked almonds
1 tsp vanilla extract
50ml apple juice
50ml pure honey
2 tbsp olive oil

Method

1. In a large bowl, toss together the rolled oats, apricots, walnuts, cranberries, almonds, vanilla extract and apple juice. Set aside.

2. Heat the honey and olive oil in a large heavy-based pan until warmed through.

3. Add the fruit and oats to the pan and bake on a low heat, stirring continually, until the oats and flaked almonds are browned.

4. Remove the from heat and allow to cool completely before decanting into an airtight container.

5. Keep in a cool dark place for up to 2 weeks.

Giving as a Gift

Sterilise 2 x 300g glass jars by placing them in a preheated oven set as low as possible for 20 minutes. Remove from the oven and allow to cool before filling with the cooled granola mix.

Using scallop-edge scissors, cut a circle of fabric slightly larger than the lid and place over the jar. Fasten in place with either decorative ribbon or band. Add a homemade tag with the list of ingredients and directions for use.

How to make a gift tag, see page 151.

Piccalilli
MAKES 4 X 500ML JARS

The delicious, sweet yet tart tang of this piccalilli makes it a condiment that, once tried, will not be beaten! A spicy and colourful way to ensure a portion of your five a day!

Ingredients

2l cold water
125g table salt
400g cauliflower florets
2 whole cucumbers, evenly diced
200g carrots, diced
200g green beans, diced
200ml malt vinegar
200ml white wine vinegar
60g caster sugar
1 tsp pickling spice
55g butter, softened
4 tbsp plain flour
2 tsp mustard powder
1 tsp cumin
½ tsp ground black pepper

Method

1. Put the water and salt in a large bowl and add all the vegetables. Place a plate over the top and allow to stand overnight to create a salt brine.

2. The following morning, drain and rinse the vegetables thoroughly to ensure all the salt is removed.

3. Place the drained vegetables a large pan of boiling water and heat on medium for approximately 10 minutes. Remove from the heat, drain and sit to one side for the moment.

4. In a large heavy-based pan, add the vinegars, sugar and pickling spice. Bring to the boil, reduce to a simmer and heat for 15 minutes. Allow to cool.

5. Sterilise glass jars and lids in an oven set at 140°C/Gas 1 for 20 minutes.

6. In a separate pan, melt the butter then add the flour and stir thoroughly. Simmer gently for 5 minutes, taking care not to burn the flour.

7. Strain the spiced vinegar and slowly add to the butter and flour, whisking continuously. Heat for 2 minutes or until thickened. Add the remaining spices and stir well. The mustard powder will turn the liquid the familiar delicious bright yellow colour.

8. Pour the liquid over the vegetables and stir thoroughly to ensure all the vegetables are coated.

9. Decant into the sterilised jars. Can be stored for up to 12 months and the longer the jars are left unopened, the stronger the flavour will be.

Giving as a Gift

Perfect as a picnic condiment, decant into small jars and place in a hand-tied box with cheese samples and a mini bottle of wine.

The window box is the perfect wrapping for this treat – allowing the bright yellow to pop and tease the recipient of what's to follow!

How to make a hand-tied gift box, see page 173.

How to make a tall window gift box, see page 164.

Pickled Cucumber
MAKES 8 SMALL GIFT JARS OR 4 X 400G JARS

The most exciting part of eating a burger for me is wondering which bite will uncover the pickle! That sweet crunch and tart tang seem to emphasise every flavour and has me hooked until the last bite. There is nothing better than a homemade burger and now you can create that mouth-watering tingle with every one you cook!

Ingredients

1 cucumber

10 tbsp table salt

160ml distilled white vinegar

50g sugar

1 tsp white mustard seeds

½ tsp chilli flakes

1 whole dried chilli per jar (if you like it hot!)

Method

1. Slice the cucumber finely and layer in a bowl with a sprinkle of salt between each layer. Cover and leave overnight to help the salt extract a lot of the water from the cucumber.

2. The following day, rinse the cucumber through a colander with plenty of cold water to make sure all of the salt is removed.

3. Sterilise the jars by placing face down in a preheated oven at 140°C/Gas 1 for 20 minutes. Do this while you are making the pickled cucumber as it will be decanted straight into the hot jars. Never put hot liquid into cold jars or cold liquid into hot jars.

4. Put the vinegar and sugar in a heavy-based pan and slowly simmer until all of the sugar has dissolved.

5. Bring to the boil and boil for about 2 minutes, stirring occasionally. Add the mustard seeds and chilli flakes, bring back to the boil for a further 3 minutes, then allow to cool slightly before spooning carefully into the jars.

7. Depending how hot you like your pickle, decide whether or not to add the whole dried chilli to your jars. Bear in mind though, the longer the jar is left unopened … the stronger and hotter the spice will be!

8. Unopened, these sterilised jars will keep for up to 1 year. Once opened, refrigerate and use within 3 months.

Giving as a Gift

Decorative jars are available in most supermarkets and health food stores. The colours in this pickle jar really pop, so enhance the natural look of this gift by fastening a simple ribbon and name label. A small plain circle and scallop circle punch (for suppliers, see page 192) are all that are needed to create this professional-looking lid tag.

Alternatives

Instead of using chilli flakes, why not try peppercorns for a slightly milder taste. Whole pink pepper-corns look rather attractive and offer a nice alternative for those that don't like their foods too spicy.

Pickled
Chilli
Cucumbers

Rum Raisins
MAKES ENOUGH TO FILL 2 X 250G JARS

Everyone loves rum and raisin ice-cream but do you know anyone who makes their own? Just take these ingredients and transform plain old ice-cream into something extra special.

Ingredients
350g raisins
250ml clear rum
Seeds scraped out of 1 vanilla pod

Method

1. Sterilise 2 x 250g glass jars and lids in an oven set at 140°C/Gas 1 for 20 minutes.

2. In a medium-size bowl, mix together all the ingredients and allow to stand overnight so that the raisins can double in size.

3. Spoon the raisins into clean jars until almost full and top with the liquid until fully covered.

4. Store in an airtight jar for up to 1 year.

Giving as a Gift

A simple label, cloth lid and decorative tag would be perfect for this gift.

How to make a gift tag, see page 151.

Spiced Nuts
MAKES 4 X 100G JARS

This recipe contains a hint of spice, a little heat and a sugary, warm coating that melts in the mouth.

Ingredients
400g mixed whole nuts (such as brazil, pecan, walnut and cashew)
4 tbsp unsalted butter
6 tbsp light brown sugar
1 tbsp cold water
½ tsp ground cumin
½ tsp ground cinnamon
½ tsp ground cayenne pepper
Pinch of salt

Method

1. Sterilise 4 x 100g jars and lids by placing in an oven set at 140°C/Gas 1 for 20 minutes. Grease a large baking tray.

2. Place the mixed nuts in a heavy-based pan over a medium heat. Dry fry until slightly browned.

3. Add the butter and sugar to the pan and stir continuously until the sugar has dissolved.

4. Mix together the water, spices and salt and add to the pan. Stir until all the nuts have a coating of the browned spice mix.

5. Empty the contents of the pan onto the prepared baking tray and use a fork to separate as much as possible.

6. Allow to stand until completely cooled, then transfer to sterilised jars or an airtight container.

Giving as a Gift

A decorative label added to the jar is all that is needed for this treat.

Alternatively why not make a gift pouch from greaseproof paper, add a bag topper and contents list for the perfect 'I'm nuts about you' treat!

How to make a custom bag topper, see page 152.

How to make a pillow pouch, see page 156.

Spiced Red Cabbage
MAKES 3 X 250ML JARS

Something about the crunchy sweet and sour taste of pickled red cabbage keeps me coming back for more and this is what led me to create my own version. I call it Cabbage with a Kick!

Ingredients
½ red cabbage, thinly sliced
10 tbsp table salt
400ml distilled white vinegar
1 tsp white peppercorns
1 tsp five-spice powder
3 whole cloves
1 tsp light mustard seeds

Method

1. Place the red cabbage in a large bowl, covering each layer as you go with a sprinkling of salt. Cover and put to one side overnight.

2. The following day, rinse the cabbage with cold water until all the salt has been removed.

3. Sterilise the jars and lids by placing face down in a preheated oven at 140°C/Gas 1 for 20 minutes.

4. Meanwhile, place the vinegar and spices into a heavy-based saucepan and boil rapidly for about 5 minutes.

5. Add the cabbage and stir until fully covered with the vinegar and heated through.

6. Spoon the mix into the sterilised jars and make sure the cabbage is submerged in the spiced vinegar. Never put hot liquid into cold jars or cold liquid into hot jars.

Giving as a Gift

Present with a handmade label and decorative ribbon. Store in the sealed jars for up to 1 year. Once opened, refrigerate and eat within 3 months.

Spicy Tomato Chutney
MAKES 6 X 250ML JARS

This chutney really packs a punch! If you like something a little spicy with your cheeses or want to add a little heat to your meals, then this tomato chutney will hit all the right spots!

Ingredients

2kg ripe tomatoes
2 large onions, diced
4 large red peppers
3 garlic cloves
2 tsp dried chilli flakes
3 whole dried chillies
300g caster sugar
250ml red wine

Method

1. Fill a pan with boiling water, add the tomatoes and allow to sit for 10 minutes.

2. While they are soaking, dice the onions and peppers and crush the garlic.

3. Lift the tomatoes out of the water, remove the skins and chop the flesh into bite-size chunks.

4. Place all the ingredients into a large heavy-based pan and heat on a low heat until bubbling.

5. Turn the heat up to medium and heat for 15 minutes, stirring occasionally to prevent sticking, until the mixture thickens.

6. Meanwhile, sterilise the glass jars and lids in an oven set at 140°C/Gas 1 for 20 minutes.

7. Decant the chutney into the sterilised jars and allow to cool before placing in the refrigerator for up to 3 months.

Giving as a Gift

As long as this chutney is stored in a cool dark place it will keep for up to 3 months, so make ahead of time and give in a hamper with cheeses and wine for an alternative Christmas gift.

Sweet & Salty Caramel Nuts

MAKES ENOUGH TO FILL 1 X 250G JAR

This sweet and salty delight can be eaten alone or used as a topping for ice-cream, cakes and desserts.

Ingredients

8 tbsp light brown sugar

4 tbsp water

2 tbsp unsalted butter

1 tbsp sea salt

200g pecan nuts

Method

1. Line a baking tray with greaseproof paper.

2. Place the sugar, water, butter and salt in a heavy-based saucepan over a low heat and stir until melted.

3. Allow to boil for 2 minutes, turn down the heat and add the pecans.

4. Gently toss the pecans in the salty caramel and continue to stir until they are all fully covered.

5. Remove from the heat and pour onto the prepared baking tray.

6. Separate with forks and allow to cool completely before transferring to an airtight jar.

Giving as a Gift

Cut a circle of fabric and fasten to the top of the jar. Secure with a ribbon and add a swing tag to embellish.

Alternatively, make a sweet treat pouch from greaseproof paper and add a decorative topper.

How to make a sweet treat pouch, see page 166.

How to make a custom bag topper, see page 152.

Tangy Lemon Curd
MAKES ENOUGH TO FILL 3 X 250ML JARS

There is something about the insane yellow of shop-bought lemon curd that puts me off! Making your own is so easy and gives so much more taste and tang that I guarantee once you try it you will never look back!

Ingredients

4 eggs
2 egg yolks
250g caster sugar
110g butter, at room temperature
Grated zest and juice of 4 large lemons
Pinch of salt

Method

1. Sterilise 3 x 250ml glass jars and lids in a preheated oven at 140°C/Gas 1 for 20 minutes.

2. Lightly whisk the eggs and egg yolks with a fork until frothy.

3. Place the caster sugar, butter, lemon zest, zest and salt in a medium bowl over a pan of boiling water and heat until the sugar has dissolved. Do not allow the bowl to touch the water.

4. Add the eggs to the bowl and heat gently for 10 minutes, stirring all the time, until thick and glossy.

5. Remove from the heat and decant into the sterilised jars. Seal with a round of greaseproof paper and put on the lid while still warm to create an airtight seal.

6. The lemon curd can be kept in a cool dry place for up to 3 months. Once opened, keep refrigerated and eat within 14 days.

Giving as a Gift

Present these curds with a pretty 'Handmade by' label and expiry date added to the front of each jar. Cut a circle of fabric with zig zag scissors and place over the lid of the jar, and fasten in place with ribbon or decorative band for that vintage look.

Whole Grain Mustard

A mix of a few standard ingredients and some of my favourite herbs and spices makes this a slightly sweet and very tasty addition to any sandwich or meat dish – even I can't get enough of it! Use it to make Honey Mustard Dressing on page 126.

Ingredients

100ml water
50g mustard powder
25g light mustard seeds
150ml dry white wine
125ml white vinegar
25g brown sugar
25g finely chopped onion
1/2 tsp turmeric
1 tsp cinnamon
3 whole allspice
½ tsp salt
1 egg yolk, lightly beaten

Method

1. Sterilise 2 x 100g glass jars and lids in a preheated oven at 140°C/Gas 1 for 20 minutes.

2. Mix the water, mustard powder and mustard seeds to a paste in a bowl and leave to stand until needed.

3. Place the dry white wine, vinegar, brown sugar, onion spices and salt in a pan and boil for approximately 10 minutes. Stir occasionally to prevent sticking.

4. Remove from the heat and strain until you have a smooth liquid.

5. Stir the hot mixture into the mustard paste in the bowl and then transfer the combined mixture back to the pan.

6. Heat until the mustard starts to thicken, then add the lightly beaten egg yolk and cook for a further 2 minutes. Remove from the heat.

7. Leave to stand for 5 minutes before decanting into the sterilised jars.

8. Store in the refrigerator and use within a month.

Giving as a Gift

Add a strip of patterned paper and a handwritten label to the storage jar for that personal touch. A small container filled with mustard would make a great addition to a personalised picnic gift set.

Empty lip balm containers are available from most chemists and online homemade cosmetic firms, which make a nice container for this condiment.

How to make a jar label, see page 151.

Alternatives

If you would prefer smoother mustard, wait until the mixture has cooled and spoon it into a food blender. Blitz on high speed for 2 minutes, scraping down if necessary, to break down all of the mustard grains.

Try adding peppercorns instead of allspice for a slightly milder taste.

Add garlic powder instead of cinnamon for a slightly less sweet kick.

6
Bottles

This chapter covers everything you need for the young and old. For the young-at-heart there is a delicious chocolate sauce that hardens on contact with ice-cream – simply magic! For those who like their gifts with a little more punch, there is a candy-flavoured vodka and raspberry-infused gin!
Add a unique label or a handmade tag. You'll find templates on page 151.

Candy Vodka
MAKES A 250ML BOTTLE

Add a sweet and colourful kick to a party staple – wow your friends with an easy-to-make homemade tipple!

Ingredients
For the vodka:
1 family size bag of Skittles
35cl bottle of good-quality vodka
For presentation:
1l airtight jar
250ml presentation bottle
Coffee filter paper or muslin

Method

1. Start by separating all the colours of Skittles. You will end up with 5 different options for your candy vodka. I worked on both red and purple in the same jar – the more candy you add, the sweeter the vodka will become.

2. If working with a different colour, remember that green leaves a bitter taste so take those out unless you like a slightly sour tang!

3. Place the chosen colour Skittles into the bottom of the airtight jar and pour in half the bottle of vodka. Fasten the jar and shake occasionally over the next day or two where the skittles will dissolve and leave a crystallised layer of sugar on the top of the vodka.

4. Line a funnel with either coffee filter paper or muslin and place in the neck of the presentation bottle. Carefully sift out all of the crystals, leaving a coloured but clear candy vodka.

Giving as a Gift

Fasten with a decorative ribbon and label: 'Please drink responsibly'.

Homemade Lemonade
SERVES 8

Forget the artificially bubbly lemonade you buy in stores. Imagine the little wooden stalls of homemade lemonade sold by roadsides in rural America, grab a paper straw, sit back and enjoy the sweetness!

Ingredients
250ml water
150g caster sugar
grated juice and zest of 8 lemons
1l cold water
Ice and lemon slices, to decorate

Method

1. Put the 250ml of water and the caster sugar in a heavy-based pan and heat gently until all the sugar has melted and a syrup starts to form.

2. Add the juice and zest of the lemons to the pan and heat through.

3. Sieve the syrup through a colander to remove all pieces of lemon zest.

4. Allow to cool before adding the cold water.

5. Decant into bottles, seal and store in the refrigerator for up to 3 days.

Giving as a Gift

A pretty ribbon wrapped around the bottles would make a simple yet effective solution to packaging. Fasten a paper straw and cocktail umbrella to the bottle for a little reminder of the good old days!

Limoncello
MAKES ABOUT 2L

A simple drink to make, but it packs a punch so make sure you serve it in small quantities!

Ingredients
500g caster sugar
700ml boiling water
Zest of 5 large lemons, grated or pared into strips
1l bottle vodka

Method

1. Sterilise a 2l glass jar and lid in a preheated oven at 140°C/Gas 1 for 20 minutes.

2. Place the sugar and boiling water in a heavy-based pan and heat gently until all the sugar has dissolved.

3. Leave to cool.

4. Whilst the sugar is dissolving, add the lemon zest to the sterilised jar and pour in the vodka.

5. Pour the sugar syrup over the lemon zest and vodka in the jar. Seal and shake well.

6. Leave in a cool, dark place for 2 weeks, then shake well again. Repeat this for 2 months, shaking every 2 weeks until the zest has lost all its colour.

7. Sterilise 2 1l bottles using the same method as above.

8. Sieve the limoncello before decanting into the bottles.

9. Store in a cool dark place and use as a liqueur or grown up lemon sauce for icecream/sorbet.

Giving as a Gift

Place one of the bottles inside the tall window box and wrap with lemon ribbon for a grown-up gift!

How to make a tall window box, see page 164.

Raspberry Gin
MAKES A 75CL BOTTLE

When you are over-run with fresh raspberries, this makes a delicious sweet and tart liqueur.

Ingredients
200g granulated sugar
450g fresh raspberries
75cl bottle good-quality gin

Method

1. Add the ingredients to a 2l jar and shake every day for 1 month.

2. Shake once a week for the next 2 months.

3. Sieve the contents through muslin and pour into a decorative bottle.

4. Serve as a liqueur.

Giving as a Gift

A simple handwritten label is all that is needed to add the finishing touch.

Magic Shell Chocolate Sauce
SERVES 4

This is guaranteed to be a winning gift with both adults and children!

Ingredients
250g milk chocolate chips
120g solid coconut oil

Method

1. Place both ingredients in a heatproof bowl over a pan of boiling water. Stir continuously until melted.

2. Pour into a microwavable glass jar and keep in the refrigerator for up to 1 week.

3. To reheat and use, simply pop in the microwave for 1 minute until runny.

4. Pour over ice-cream, then watch the sauce harden to a shell over the cold ice-cream!

Giving as a Gift

The ideal packaging for this sauce is either microwaveable glass jars or squeezy bottles. Wash out old condiment jars and bottles, then decant the sauce directly from the pan. Allow to cool before decorating with a sticky label and use-by date. Wrap with ribbon and attach a decorative toffee hammer to help break the 'shell'.

Salad Dressings

EACH ONE MAKES ABOUT 300ML

Liven up a plain and boring salad!
Here are 5 examples of easy-to-make and delicious-to-eat salad dressings.

Classic Vinaigrette

6 tsp Dijon mustard
6 tbsp white wine vinegar
12 tbsp olive oil

Honey Mustard Dressing

6 tsp Dijon mustard
6 tbsp balsamic vinegar
6 tbsp pure honey
12 tbsp olive oil

Garlic & Herb Dressing

10 tbsp olive oil
2 garlic cloves, crushed
2 tsp chopped fresh herbs
3 tbsp white wine vinegar
2 tbsp fresh lemon juice

Yogurt & Honey Dressing

3 tbsp natural yogurt
4 tbsp olive oil
4 tbsp pure honey
4 mint leaves
2 tbsp lemon juice

Balsamic Dressing

4 tbsp cider vinegar
4 tbsp balsamic vinegar
8 tbsp olive oil
2 tbsp caster sugar
1 tsp soy sauce

Method

1. Use the same method for each dressing.

2. Place all the ingredients into a jar, put on the lid tightly and shake vigorously.

3. Pour over salad as needed.

4. The dressings will keep in the refrigerator for up to 5 days.

Giving as a Gift

Decorative glass jars look great fastened with a single ribbon and swing tag. To brighten them up a little, create one-of-a-kind artworks with glass paint. Write the recipient's name, special occasion date and type of dressing on the front of the bottle to make it a gift to remember.

How to make a gift tag, see page 151.

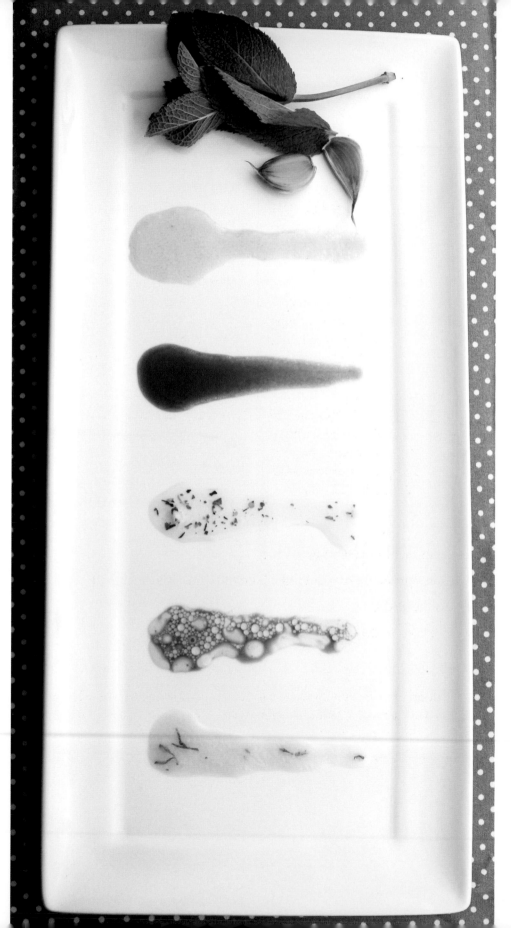

Summer Berry Sauce
SERVES 8

This delightful jewel-red sauce is a wonderful topping for ice-cream! It works great as a cupcake filling too.

Ingredients
200g caster sugar
100ml water
250g strawberries, sliced
100g blueberries
100g raspberries
1 tbsp red wine
Grated zest of 1 orange
Grated zest and juice of 1 lemon

Method

1. Put the caster sugar and water in a heavy-based saucepan and heat gently until the sugar has melted.

2. Pour in the strawberries, blueberries and raspberries and coat with the sugary syrup.

3. Stir in the red wine, orange zest and lemon zest and juice and continue stirring until the sauce starts to thicken.

4. Simmer for 10 minutes until a thick syrup consistency is achieved. Remove from the heat and allow to cool.

5. Sterilise some glass jars and lids in a preheated oven at 140°C/Gas 1 for 20 minutes.

6. Decant the sauce into the sterilised glass jars.

7. Spoon over ice-cream while warm or store in a refrigerator until needed.

8. Can be re-heated before using.

Giving as a Gift

The paper basket created within this book is an ideal packaging idea for this sauce. Stack alongside fresh fruits and a decorative spoon for a wonderful summer fruits gift!

How to make a paper basket, see page 154.

7
All Sorts

We like to take care of the outside as well as the inside so what better to give than gifts where you know every single ingredient included. Each recipe is filled with natural contents, with no preservatives, just pure ingredients that will cleanse and smooth the skin. Go one step further and create simple handmade decorations to scent the home. Give them as gifts in a unique box with a handmade tag. You'll find hints and templates on page 151.

Brown Sugar Body Scrub
MAKES 400ML

A sweet treat for dry skin!

Ingredients
400g brown sugar
20ml good-quality olive oil
5 tbsp pure honey
1 tsp vanilla extract or other essential oil

Method

1. Combine all the ingredients in a medium bowl and stir until fully combined.

2. Decant into a decorative jar and store in a cool, dark place for up to 2 months.

Giving as a Gift

There are so many pretty glass jars on the market. With the fashion for make do and mend being in the forefront of everyone's mind why not scour charity shops for a pretty container.

Fasten with a ribbon and add a sticky label for a handmade treat at a fraction of the price of a store-bought jar.

Coconut Body Butter

This thick butter contains coconut oil which turns to liquid with body heat. A fresh alternative to store-bought, additive-laden lotions.

Ingredients

175ml olive oil

60g coconut oil (solid)

30g shea butter

25g beeswax

3 drops of coconut essential oil

Method

1. In a large microwaveable bowl, melt together the olive oil, solid coconut oil, shea butter and beeswax. Stir at 1-minute intervals until fully dissolved.

2. Once fully melted, remove from the microwave and add the drops of coconut oil.

3. Using a hand blender, blitz the mixture on high for 2 minutes. The mixture will become cloudy at this point.

4. The butter will start to set, so pour immediately into a decorative glass jar and leave to cool.

5. Leave to solidify overnight before use.

6. Label and refrigerate for up to 3 months.

Giving as a Gift

Present in the paper gift basket with a sample of the rose hand cream and oat body scrub for a perfect body care gift.

How to make the paper basket, see page 154.

How to make Rose Hand Cream, see page 140.

How to make Oat Body Scrub, see page 136.

Coconut Body Balm
MAKES 4 X 75ML JARS

No additives, no colours, no hard-to-pronounce ingredients! Just a simple lotion that works wonders on dry skin and can be made at home in 5 minutes. A natural way to healthy, great-looking skin.

Ingredients
30g beeswax
100ml coconut oil
120ml cocoa butter
50ml almond oil

Method

1. Place the beeswax in a microwavable container and heat for 30-second intervals on high until all the beads have dissolved.

2. Remove from the microwave and add the remaining ingredients.

3. Using a food processor or blender attachment, blitz on high for 2 minutes until the mix is thick and creamy.

4. Decant into sterilised jars and use within 18 months.

Giving as a Gift

Decant into small jars and wrap together with the lip scrub (page 146) and body scrub (page 131) for a perfect skin care gift. Stacked together in the tall window box and finished with a decorative ribbon and swing tag, you have an expensive-looking gift for a fraction of the price of a store-bought alternative.

How to make tall window gift box, see page 164.

Oat Body Scrub

MAKES A 300ML JAR

This soft and delicate scrub is ideal for even the most sensitive of skins.

Ingredients

100g coconut oil (solid)
20ml olive oil
150g dried porridge oats
3 tbsp pure honey

Method

1. Put the coconut oil and olive oil in a medium microwaveable bowl. Heat on high power for 2 minutes, stirring at 30-second intervals, until fully dissolved.

2. Remove from the microwave and stir in the porridge oats and honey.

3. Allow to soak overnight before using.

4. To use, scoop a small amount of the oat mix into a loofa and bush onto wet skin.

Giving as a Gift

Simple is perfect for this gift. Using a small amount of thin baking string or baker's twine, available from craft stores, fasten a small piece of loofa sponge to the jar and pop inside the self-fastening box.

How to make a self-fastening box, see page 175.

Orange & Cinnamon Hangers
MAKES 3

Everyone loves the smell of cinnamon around the home. Add to it the citrus smell of dried orange slices and you have an intoxicating aroma that makes it feel like Christmas all year round.

Ingredients
3 large oranges, thinly sliced

12 cinnamon sticks

36 bay leaves

Twine to hang

Method

1. Preheat the oven to the lowest setting and arrange the orange slices on 3 large baking trays.

2. Heat for at least 3 hours, turning occasionally to ensure they dry throughout.

3. Remove from the oven and allow to cool fully before assembling hangers.

4. Knot the twine to prevent it slipping through the cinnamon sticks and thread onto a large eye needle.

5. Start by threading the cinnamon stick, then 2 bay leaves, followed finally by an orange slice. Repeat until you have the desired length.

6. Fasten the twine into a loop to hang.

Giving as a Gift

These make ideal tags to hang from Christmas presents, something you can guarantee no one else will have thought of!

Simply wrap in tissue paper and place inside the tied gift box – fasten with citrus-coloured ribbon and sprinkle with orange essential oil for an effective (and scented) gift!

How to make a self-fastening gift box, see page 175.

Rose Hand Cream
MAKES 1 X 200ML JAR

An old favourite that is making a revival, roses are popular with shabby chic enthusiasts and romantics the world over.

Ingredients

75g coconut oil (solid)

75ml olive oil

2 drops of pink soap colouring

6 drops of rose water

Method

1. Put the coconut oil and olive oil in a medium bowl and microwave on high, stirring at 1-minute intervals, until fully dissolved.

2. Remove from the microwave and stir in the colouring and rose water.

3. Using a hand blender, blitz on high for 2 minutes until smooth and creamy.

4. Decant into a decorative glass jar.

5. Allow to set for a minimum of 2 hours before use.

6. Use within 3 months.

Giving as a Gift

This hand cream is the ideal opportunity to make a heartfelt gift that will provoke memories and become a keepsake!

Fasten with ribbon and decorative antique key or pearls.

Stack in a tower with the oat body scrub and coconut body butter for the ultimate skin care gift set!

Rose Petal Soap
MAKES 25 SLICES

Nothing evokes memories more than power of scent. Present this gift to a loved one, delicately wrapped in paper and fastened with twine, and know those memories last for ever.

Ingredients

50g dried rose petals

1kg melt-and-pour soap base

1 tbsp rose water

Method

1. Prepare a 20cm silicone deep dish baking tray by sprinkling the dried rose petals to cover the bottom.

2. Place the melt-and-pour soap base in a large microwaveable bowl. Heat on high for 5 minutes. Remove and stir. Repeat this process at minute intervals until the soap base has completely melted. Stir in the rose water.

3. Pour the melted soap into the silicone tray. The roses will float to the top.

4. Allow to set overnight before slicing with a large, sharp knife.

Giving as a Gift

Wrap in greaseproof paper with a decorative paper outer wrap. Fasten with twine.

The mini pizza box would make a perfect container for this gift – you could even decorate the soap and box to match the 'flavour' of pizza you are giving.

How to make a pizza box, see page 170.

Alternatives

Create a selection of different scented soaps by using fresh ingredients. Mint leaves give a delicious fresh aroma. Oats will work as an exfoliant and fresh aloe will add soothing properties.

Embed lemon slices in the soap as soon as it is poured to create capsules of tangy freshness.

Sicilian Orange & Wheatgerm Soap

MAKES 25 SLICES

This adorable soap is a perfect gift! Made to look like a cheesecake with a biscuit base and fresh fruit topping, both foodies and cosmetic lovers alike will just love it.

Ingredients
1.2kg melt-and-pour soap base
50g organic wheatgerm
6 dried orange slices
Sicilian orange essence oil

Method

1. In a large bowl, heat the melt-and-pour soap base in a microwave on high, stirring at minute intervals, until fully dissolved.

2. Place the wheatgerm, as a layer, in the bottom of a silicone loaf tin.

3. Pour the melted soap base into the loaf tin and stir to ensure the wheatgerm is evenly mixed throughout the soap. (The wheatgerm will give a yellow colour and settle at the bottom to create the 'biscuit base').

4. Whilst the soap is still liquid, place the orange slices on top and press lightly to ensure they set within the soap.

5. Add a drop of orange oil to the top of each orange slice.

6. Leave for 2 hours to set and cool completely.

7. Turn out onto a clean work surface. Cut with a large, greased knife and wrap individually in cellophane to present.

Giving as a Gift

Wrap each slice of soap, separately, in a small doily, before tying with string and a name label. Pop into a cellophane bag and seal with a sticky label.

Alternatively, wrap in cellophane and place inside the pizza box for the perfect presentation idea!

How to make a pizza box, see page 170.

Alternatives

Dried lavender, lemon slices, dried rose petals or buds, oatmeal (which will act as a body scrub), and any dried flowers and herbs will all work with this soap.

So Sweet Lip Scrub
MAKES 2 X 10 ML POTS

Kissable lips are a must – this scrub will make sure you have the softest lips in town!

Ingredients

½ tsp olive oil

1 tsp pure honey

2 tsp brown sugar

2 drops of essential oil (peppermint, lemon, rose)

Method

1. Mix all the ingredients together in a small bowl.

2. Spoon carefully into an empty lip balm pot or small airtight container.

3. To use, remove a small amount and rub on the lips. Rinse and apply homemade lip-balm.

Giving as a Gift

Sealed in an airtight container, this lip scrub will last 2 months.

Make a selection of different flavours and stack them together in the double-ended box or window box.

How to make a double-ended gift box, see page 182.

How to make a tall window gift box, see page 164.

Soothing Avocado Face Mask
ENOUGH FOR 1 APPLICATION

Fresh, soothing and gentle, this face mask will revitalise tired-looking skin.

Ingredients
1 small avocado
2 tbsp pure honey

Method

1. Peel and de-stone the avocado.

2. Using the back of a fork, crush the avocado to a pulp, then blend in the honey.

3. Apply to the face, avoiding the eyes. Leave for 10 minutes, then wash off with warm water.

Giving as a Gift

This is ideal for a night in with the girls! Invite your friends for a treat. Play a movie, paint your nails and, while waiting for them to dry, pop two sliced of cucumber on your eyes, lie back and try out this calming mask.

8
Packaging Ideas

There is a reason we go window shopping. It is to take a peek at what is in store for us should we venture into the shop.

Think of packaging in the same way, a simple box fastened with ribbons and dainty embellished tags entices your recipient to take their time over unwrapping and discovering what is inside. If you choose a window box, it gives a little sneak preview as to what they will receive.

Anticipation and presentation should be at the top of a gift-giver's list of must-have items!

Basic equipment

For most projects, you will need the following basic equipment.

• Double-sided tape • Pencil • Ruler • Scissors • Scoring tool • Writing pen

Everything else you will need for the project is listed at the beginning of the instructions. If you do not have a local supplier, you can buy online from the suppliers listed on page 192 or ask them for advice.

Chipboard is used for backing picture frames and is available from the craft suppliers or from picture framers. It is thicker and stronger than card.

Cardstock varies in weight from 210–290gsm but needs to be thick enough to keep the box stiff and stable.

Wet glue: I use Ranger Glossy Accent.

Gift Tags

Use tracing paper to draw around the template and copy on to patterned paper or card. Or simply use as a guide to measure and draw templates of your own from the ideas shown in this section. Cut around your template and adhere to packaging or punch a small hole in one corner and attach to your gift with ribbons.

Custom Bag Topper

These handy bag toppers an be used as a decorative seal for cellophane bags or plain paper gift bags. They can be used and adapted for any occasion. The decoration is entirely up to you – why not add dried flowers, crystals, a little photograph or even instructions on how to make what is included in the bag.

You will need your basic equipment plus:
* Cardstock
* Decorative border punch
* Stapler
* Patterned paper
* Hole punch
* Ribbon

Step One. Cut a piece of cardstock that is the correct width and twice the required height of the bag you are to use as a gift bag.

Step Two. Score in the middle and press firmly to create a sharp crease.

Step Three. Use the border punch to create a decorative edge.

Step Four. Staple the bag topper in place.

Step Five. Cut the patterned paper to the correct size and adhere to the front of the bag topper with double-sided tape. Cut a small blank tag from the remaining cardstock and write your message. Punch 2 small holes and fasten with ribbon.

Paper Basket

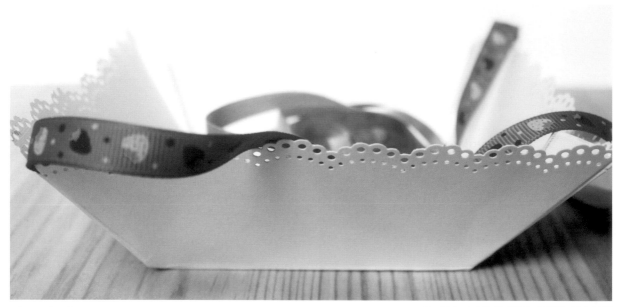

The ideal presentation for sweets treats or candy, stack the sweets high in the basket and wrap with cellophane, then fasten with ribbons for a beautiful gift.

You will need your basic equipment plus:
- 20x20cm white cardstock
- Decorative edge punch (optional)

Step One. Draw lines from each corner to mark the centre point.

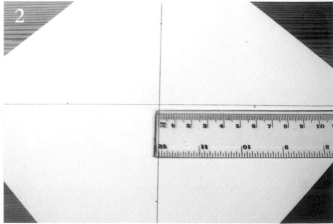

Step Two. From the centre mark, measure 6cm and draw a mark on each line.

Step Three. Using the ruler, draw lines to join up these marks to create a square base.

Step Four. Using the scoring tool, make a mark and score a line 2.5cm from each corner of the cardstock to edge of the square you just made.

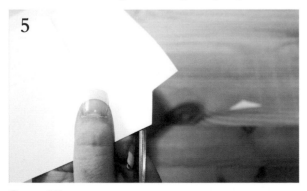

Step Five. Snip the corner of your cardstock away and discard.

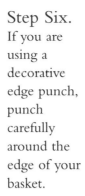

Step Six. If you are using a decorative edge punch, punch carefully around the edge of your basket.

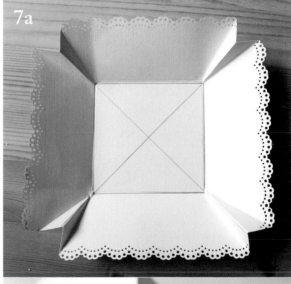

Step Seven. Place double-sided tape on the underside of each scored corner section and press together to seal.

Pillow Pouch

Everyone loves a chocolate … or two! Pillow pouches are the ideal way to hide a surprise treat!

You will need your basic equipment plus:
- 20.5x20.5cm piece of cardstock
- Compact disk (to draw around)
- Decorations and embellishments

Step One. Start by drawing lines at 10cm and 20cm.

Step Two. Score and fold these lines to create a sharp crease.

Step Three. Hold the cd at the top of the cardstock and draw around to create an arc.

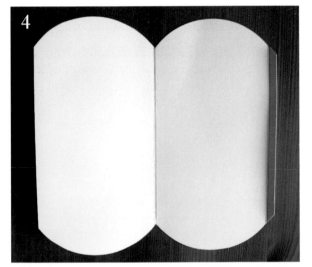

Step Four. Cut away the excess cardstock.

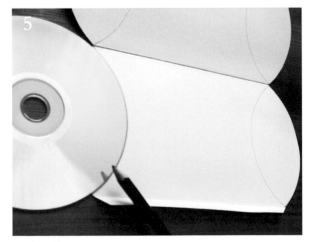

Step Five. Move the cd so that it is level with the edges of the arc just drawn. Score this section to create the fold needed for the end of the pouch.

Step Six. Place double-sided tape on the tab and press into place to secure.

Step Seven. Fold the ends of the pouch in on themselves to create a seal. Simply fasten with ribbon to create a sweet treat holder.

Cupcake Window Box

This is a useful little box for all kinds of treats. A little glimpse at what's in store makes this the packaging perfect for delicious cupcakes and mini delights.

You will need your basic equipment plus:
- Paper trimmer
- Ruler
- 1 21x29cm piece of cardstock

- Acetate
- Scoring tool
- Scissors
- Double-sided sticky tape runner
- Ribbon

(optional extras – *decorative edge punch, embellishments)

*See list on page 192 for recommended stockists

Step One. Start by working in portrait position. Score and fold the card at 1cm, 7cm, 13cm and 20cm.

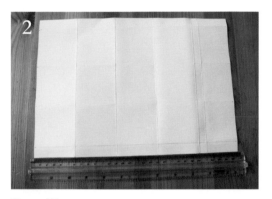

Step Two. Turn clockwise and score lines and fold crisply at 12cm, 14cm, 18cm 24cm and 25cm.

Step Three. Cut away all of the sections shown in the photograph above to create the box body.

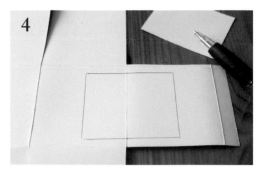

Step Four. To create the acetate window, cut a rectangle of card to measure 10x5cm. Place on the underside of the lid and draw around.

Step Five. Carefully cut out this rectangle and discard centre. Cut the acetate to 11x6cm and, using the double sided tape, add a little adhesive around the window. Press firmly on the acetate to secure.

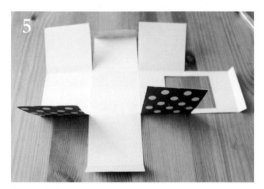

Step Six. Place double sided tape on the side panels and fold to secure. Press firmly to secure the box. You now have the finished basics of a rectangle window box. Decorate as required.

Milk Carton

A novel way to present cookies, stack 'em high and watch the smiles appear when you present your handmade treats in this unique way. You can decorate the carton how you like, then add a swing tag for your message.

You will need your basic equipment plus:
- A4 piece of cardstock
- Bulldog clip/mini pegs
- Decorations and embellishments

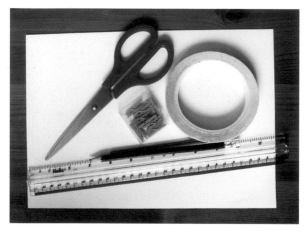

Step One. Work with the long side of your card facing you and score at 7cm, 14cm, 21cm and 28cm. Turn the card 90 degrees and score at 6cm, 14cm and 19.5cm.

Step Two. Fold and press firmly to ensure the creases are sharp.

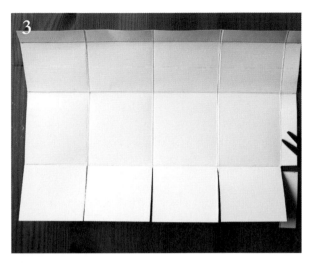

Step Three. Cut into the base section of the milk carton and completely remove the small extra section at the right-hand side.

Step Four. Place double-sided tape onto the small tab section and fold over to create a tube.

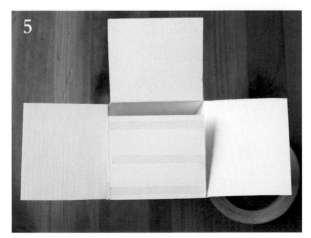

Step Five. To create the base, fold in 1 of the tabs and fold the other 3 outwards. Add double-sided tape to the tab folded inwards.

Step Six. Fold one of the other base tabs over, press to secure and add double-sided tape to this tab. Repeat until all the base tabs are folded and pressed together.

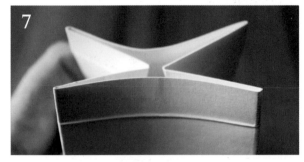

Step Seven. Stand the milk carton upright and pinch the edges so that the 2 short score lines are folded inwards towards the centre of the box.

Step Eight. Secure the top section with pegs or a bulldog clip to ensure all of the folds are sharp. To finish, simply punch 2 holes in the top and fasten with a ribbon and swing tag, adding any decorations you wish.

Mini Sweet Gift Bag

What party would be complete without a goodie bag and what better than a handmade bag to go with the treats! These adorable little bags are also the perfect size to turn into advent gifts or tree decorations – tie them in with each celebration.

You will need your basic equipment plus:
- 30x30cm piece of cardstock
- Paper trimmer
- Scallop punch
- Decorations and embellishments

Step One.
Cut a piece of card for the main bag 20x10cm. Turn

it so that the short side is facing you and score at 2.5cm in from either side. Turn again so the long side is facing you and score at 8, 10 and 12 cm from the left-hand side. Fold and cut little triangles from the 8cm and 12 cm marks.

Step Two.
Place double-sided tape on the bottom and a very small strip on the right-hand

side folds. Fold in the side panel that has the double-sided tape first, then stick to the bottom/side panel.

Step Three.
Bring up the other side and fold this over the thin strip – you will notice at this point

the box is tapering in at the top.

Step Four. Cut your co-ordinating paper 8x20cm and scallop one long edge.

Step Five. Score the paper 2.5cm in from the opposite end to the scallops.

Step Six. Place this on top of your box and snip a little mark where you need to score and cut.

Step Seven. Again cut little triangles either side of your score marks so that they will fold over without any bulk.

Step Eight. Make sure it is to size by folding it over the top of your bag without sticking it. Fold the sides around and nip

tightly to mark where you next need to cut.

Step Nine. Repeat for both sides and make sure you trim enough so that the back looks equal at both sides. Fasten with double-sided tape and add your chosen decorations.

Tall Window Gift Box

Just like the cupcake window box, this delightful box gives a sneak preview of what's in store. Once it is all assembled, pop in the presents you wish to give (jar, bottle, chocolates, cookies etc.) and slip on the lid. Fasten some ribbons around the lid and box itself for added decoration.

You will need your basic equipment plus:
* 28x28cm piece of cardstock
* 11.5cm square piece of cardstock
* 5x16cm piece of acetate
* Decorations and embellishments

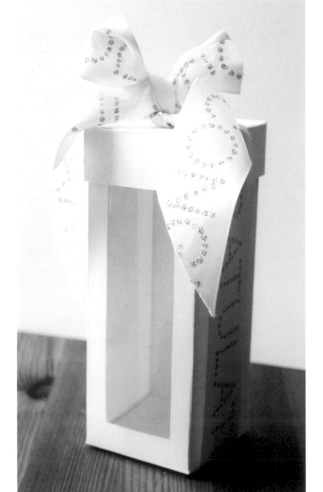

Step One. Mark lines on the cardstock at 6cm, 12cm 18cm and 24cm point, working from the left-hand side. You will be left with a 4cm strip which is the overlap to secure.

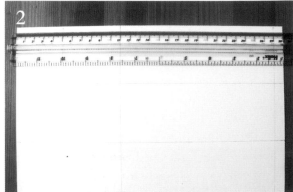

Step Two. Turn the cardstock 90 degrees clockwise and mark lines at 5cm, 11cm and 27cm.

3

4

Step Three. Notice which sections I have drawn on and do the same to yours – these sections need to be cut out and discarded.

Step Four. Remember to cut along the 2 bottom sections to allow the base to fold and adhere to the sides.

Step Six. Fold in the 2 base side panels and cut triangles from each side of the main base piece. Slot into place.

6

7

Step Seven. To make the lid, take the 11.5cm square. Score at 2.5cm in from each side.

5

Step Five. Score down all the drawn lines and make sure all the sides fold without any problem. Cut out the window which is in the front section. Leave a 1cm gap around the edge so that the acetate can be attached on the other side. Attach the acetate.

8

Step Eight. Cut slight triangles from the corners so they are tapered and will lie flat.

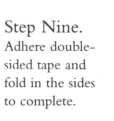

9

Step Nine. Adhere double-sided tape and fold in the sides to complete.

Sweet Treat Pouch

This neat little pouch is a simple yet decorative addition to an offering of a single cookie!

You will need your basic equipment plus:
- 30x20cm piece of cardstock
- Scallop punch
- Corner rounder
- Decorations and embellishments

Step One. Score the paper in half then move 2.5cm to the left and score again, move another 2.5cm to the left and score again. You should now have a little peak once it is folded in on itself.

Step Two. Turn the sheet over and score at 2.5cm and 5cm from the edge of the paper. You should now have two peaks when folded in.

Step Three. 10cm from the top of the paper, make a cut all the way along, through all of the peaks and folds to your initial fold line.

Step Four. Fold it all in on itself and make sure there is no overhang, if there is, trim this now as it is easier than after assembly.

Step Five. Fold the top section down to create a flap which will be stuck against the back, creating a backdrop for the goodie bag. Using a scallop punch, punch the top edge of the front pocket.

Step Six. Use a corner rounder on the corners on the top section.

Step Seven. Place double-sided tape on the 3 points shown.

Step Eight. Place double-sided tape on the bottom of the pouch and fold it all in on itself, applying pressure to secure.

Tiffany-style Gift Box

This simple and stylish little box doesn't need too much embellishment – for this, less is more. Simply tie with beautiful ribbon and add a swing tag for your message.

You will need your basic equipment plus:
- 2 x 20x20cm pieces of cardstock
- Decorations and embellishments

Step One. To create the box base, take one of the 20cm squares of cardstock and draw lines at 5cm and 15cm. Score and fold these lines.

Step Two. Turn 90 degrees and repeat step 1.

Step Three. Cut the folds to the point where they join.

Step Four. Place double-sided tape on each flap and fold in to create the box shape. Press to secure.

Step Five. Repeat for the other 3 sides and put to one side while you make the lid.

Step Six. To create the lid, take another piece of the 20cm square cardstock and draw lines at 5.2cm and 14.8cm. Score and fold these lines.

Step Seven. Turn 90 degrees and repeat step 6.

Step Eight. Cut and assemble the box lid following steps 3 to 5 for the base.

Step Nine. Fasten with ribbon and swing tag.

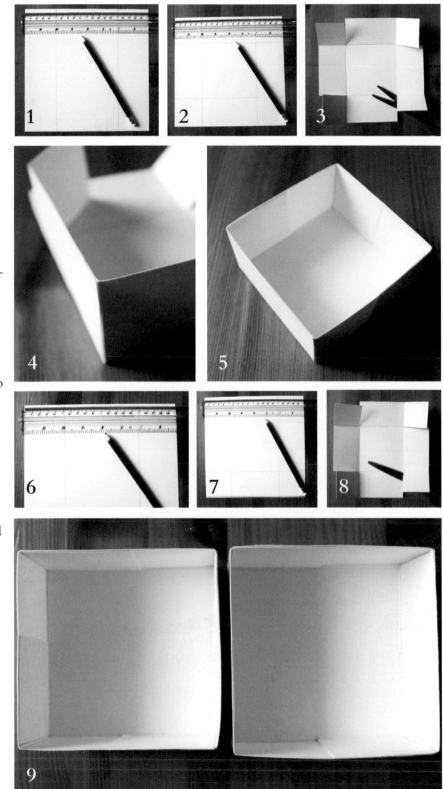

Pizza Box

Here is a great little box that you can personalise or custom design to incorporate the recipients favourite things.

You will need your basic equipment plus:
- 30x21cm piece of white cardstock
- Trimmer

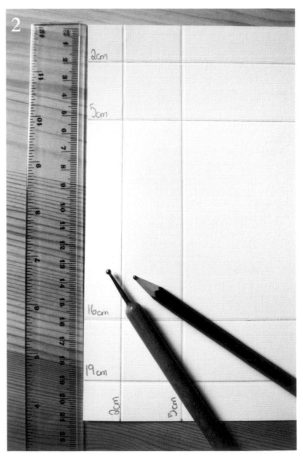

Step One. Placing your cardstock landscape in front of you, draw and score lines at 2, 5, 15, 18 and 28cm.

Step Two. Turn the cardstock portrait and draw and score lines at 2, 5, 16 and 19cm.

Step Three. Keeping the cardstock landscape, cut away and discard the sections shown.

Step Four. Cut away the two small end sections to create the lip of the box; discard these pieces. Cut to the fold in the remaining scored sections to create the side reinforcements.

Step Five. Place double-sided sticky tape onto all of the overlapping folds as shown.

Step Six. Remove sticky tape from one inner side panel at a time and fold in together to meet.

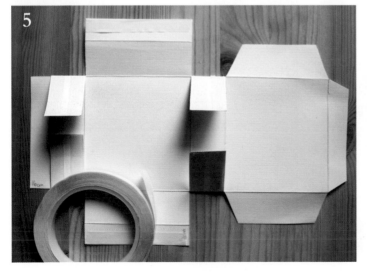

Step Seven. Fold up the outer side panel and adhere by folding over the additional crease into the box.

Step Eight. Fold in the remaining sides to create the box base.

Step Nine. The lid side panels can now be folded in on themselves and used to secure the lid in place when the box is closed. Decorate as required and fasten with ribbons or baking string.

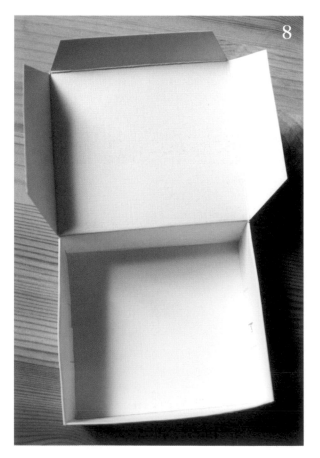

Hand-tied Gift Box

This is a simple little gift box that is ideal for those last-minute gifts. It is made in seconds but lovely to receive. Decorate to suit the recipient, pile in the gifts, then thread a length of ribbon through the two holes, fastening in a double knot.

You will need your basic equipment plus:
- 21x29cm piece of cardstock
- Hole punch
- Ribbon
- Decorations and embellishments

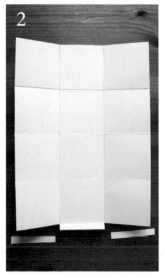

Step One. Draw a rectangle made up of three rows of 4 squares measuring 7x7cm each.

Step Two. You will be left with a 1cm strip at the end which will work as a tab to hold the sides together. Cut the top and bottom 1cm and discard. Score all the lines.

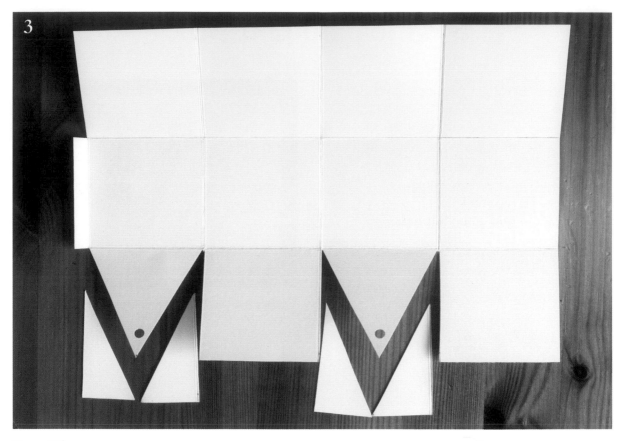

Step Three. On the second and fourth squares at the top, mark the centre points and cut away the remaining card to leave little triangles. Punch a hole into the top of each triangle.

Step Four. Place double-sided tape onto the small side lip that will fasten inside the box. Press into place to create a 'tunnel'.

Step Five. Bring up one of the base lips and place double-sided tape on the underside. Bring up the second base lip and press into place. Repeat for the rest of the base and press firmly into place.

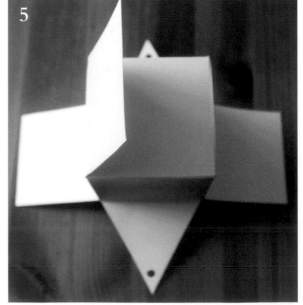

Self-fastening Gift Box

An attractive, decorative box that is perfect for male or female gifts! Tied with raffia or simply left plain, this box could be adapted for every handmade treat!

You will need your basic equipment plus:
• A4 piece of cardstock
• Decorations and embellishments

Step One. From top to bottom of the A4 card, draw lines at 1cm, 6cm, 11cm and 16cm. Score and fold to create sharp creases.

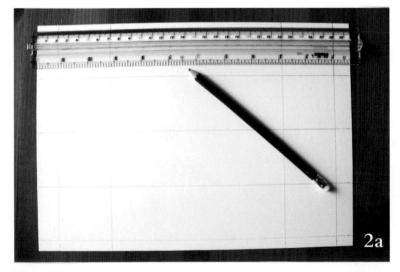

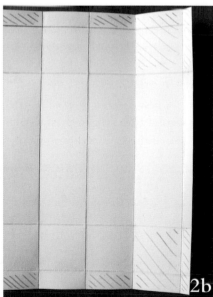

Step Two. Turn the cardstock 90 degrees and draw lines at 2cm, 7cm, 23cm and 28cm. Score and fold to create sharp creases.

Step Three. Cut and remove the sections as shown.

Step Four. Place double-sided tape onto the side tab and fold box to create a 'tunnel'. Secure the side tab in place.

Step Five. Fold in the bottom 2 flaps and secure with the tab. Fold in the top flaps and secure with the tab.

Step Six. Fasten with ribbon and a tag or decorate with patterned paper and label.

Chest of Drawers

Here is a lovely little chest of drawers for small items like sweets. Make it in colours and patterns to suit the recipient and decorate as you wish. Add lots of bling, flowers, gems and jewels or simply pop a little ribbon around the top! Fill with homemade chocolates and I am sure it will be adored by whoever receives it.

You will need your basic equipment plus:
- 29.5x10cm piece of paper
- 2.5x7cm piece of chipboard
- 4 x 5.5x7cm pieces of chipboard
- 25x7cm piece of paper
- 17x17cm piece of paper for the lid
- 2 x 15x15cm pieces of paper for the drawers

Step One. Place your longest strip of paper face down and, starting from the left-hand side, stick your smallest strip of cardstock onto the paper with double-sided tape. Leave a small gap between each one and place each of the 4 larger pieces alongside, so that the card does not tear when folded.

Step Two. Put double-sided tape all around the outside of the remaining paper as this needs to be folded over. Fold the corners over first to ensure a neat finish. Then fold over all of the sides and make sure you press firmly, making sure your box will bend at each of the spaces between the cardstock.

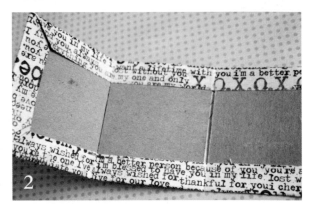

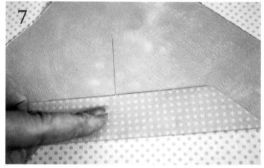

Step Three. Cover your slightly smaller strip of paper in double-sided tape and place this over the top of the pieces you have just turned over – this gives a neat and perfect finish to the inside of your box.

Step Four. Again make sure it all folds neatly without any blisters and press down ensuring all the double-sided tape is in place.

Step Five. You are going to do the same for the inside drawers as you are about to do for the lid so please refer back to this part and simply redo for the drawers.
Place a ruler onto each adjacent corner and draw a line across the middle point of your paper – turn and do the same again so you have a cross in the middle.

Step Six. Fold each corner in to touch the centre point.

Step Seven. Fold this section again, making sure you stay on the line in the centre. Do this for each side.

Step Eight. Make cuts down 2 adjacent folds giving you 2 sections with arms and 2 without.

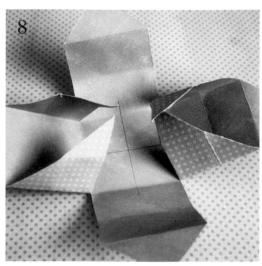

9

10

11

Step Nine. Fold the sides with the arms up and bring the folds over into the centre to reinforce the other sides.

Step Ten. Now fold the last bit up and over. A little sticky tape on the end of this piece may be needed to hold it in place.

12

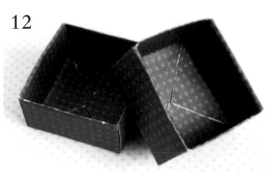

13

Step Eleven. Repeat for the other side.

Step Twelve. Repeat steps 5 to 11 for the 2 internal drawers.

Step Thirteen. Place a little double-sided tape onto one side of each drawer.

14

Step Fourteen. Stick one drawer onto the bottom of the last section of your box and the other drawer onto the top of the middle section.

Step Fifteen. The lid will be a tight fit at first but this eases up after the first fitting. You need it secure to hold the box together. The bottom drawer should be level with the bottom of the box so that when anything is placed in the drawer it will not sag.

15

Coffee Treats Box

The patterned paper I used for my box is the Bitty dots from Papertrey Ink (see page 192). Instead of cutting the rectangle in the top of the box, I punched out small circles and used the scallop punch to create small frames around these circles.

I decorated my treats box with ribbon (From my Kitchen with Love) and used the little coffee cup from the Warm Happiness stamps and the small Enjoy stamp from the Tags for Spring set to create a background paper. The large Enjoy is from the Spiral Bouquet set and the coffee cups are from Warm Happiness – all by Papertrey Ink.

You will need your basic equipment plus:
- A4 sheet of white cardstock
- Decorations and embellishments

Step One. Take the sheet of cardstock and score at 2cm, 4cm, 10.5cm, 12.5cm and 23cm.

Step Two. Turn the cardstock and score at 2cm, 4cm, 17cm and 19cm.

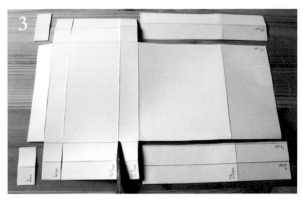

Step Three. Cut away and discard the corner pieces as shown.

Step Five. Bring both side reinforcement pieces in together and fold over the actual side panel. Do the same for both sides as you need both in place before you bring up the back panel.

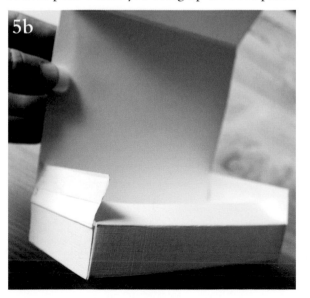

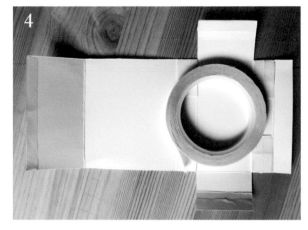

Step Four. Stick double-sided tape to the pieces as shown in the photograph. All are on the 'right' side of the panels as they are all to be brought up and secured together.

Step Six. Cut the top section from the box to enable biscuits, candy, lollies and so on to stand upright.

Step Seven. Bring up the back panel and secure with the double-sided tape that is exposed. Press firmly to secure.

Double-ended Gift Box

This simplest of boxes can be made in a myriad sizes depending on the treat to be given. From cookies to hanging room fresheners, this container would be perfect to hold them all! Use plain or patterned card, pretty ribbon and a homemade tag.

You will need your basic equipment plus:
- 2 x 20x20cm pieces of cardstock for the ends
- 1 x 22x22cm piece of cardstock for the insert
- Decorations and embellishments

Step One. You need to make two identical box ends. Take one of your 20cm square piece of cardstock. Find the centre point by drawing a line from opposite corners.

Step Two. Fold each corner to the point where your lines cross in the middle.

Step Three. While the corner is still touching the centre point, fold the section again so that it is now doubled over and along the pencil line. Repeat for all corners.

Step Four. Unfold all the sections and you will have a square in the middle that is not folded. With one of the corners facing you, cut through the sections from the start of the first fold and down to the start of the flat box. Do this on 2 opposite sides only.

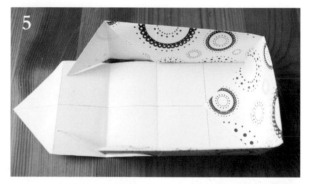

Step Five. Fold the uncut sides into the middle of the box to create the sides. Tuck the sides of these pieces into the box to create a makeshift side panel and fold the 'cut' side piece over this to create the actual side of the box. Repeat procedeure for second box end.

Step Six. To make the inside lining section, take the 22cm piece of cardstock. Score the cardstock at 5cm intervals. This will leave a 2cm piece to overlap and fasten into a square. Place double-sided tape around the outside of the bottom of the insert. Place inside the bottom box shell and press firmly to secure on all taped sections.

Step Seven. Fill with goodies and pop the lid on top. Decorate simply or make it as fancy as you like.

Old-fashioned Chocolate Box

Bring back the romance of a gift of chocolates with this decorative gift box. Women would keep chocolate boxes in years gone by, the boxes were simply so much prettier than mass made ones! Make the packaging as important as the contents!

You will need your basic equipment plus:
- Large cardboard tubes or inner card rings from sticky tape
- White cardstock
- Patterned paper
- Wet glue (I use Ranger Glossy Accent, available from the craft stores listed on page 192)
- Ribbon
- Compasses or CD
- Decorations and embellishments

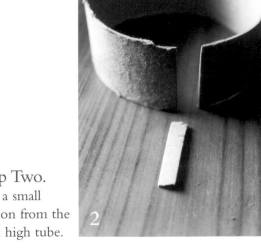

Step One. If you are using the large cardboard tubes, cut down to 6cm and 3cm lengths.

Step Two. Cut a small section from the 3cm high tube.

Step Three. Glue or tape the edges together to create a smaller tube.

Step Four. Draw around the CD or use the compass to create 2 circles on which the tubes will sit.

Step Five. Cover the circles and tubes with patterned paper.

Step Six. Using the wet glue, stick the tubes on to the decorative circles.

Step Seven. Allow to set before filling with cookies or candy. Decorate as required and finish with ribbon to seal.

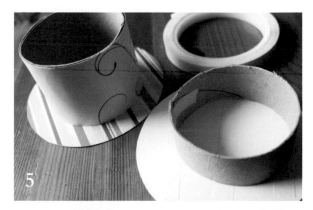

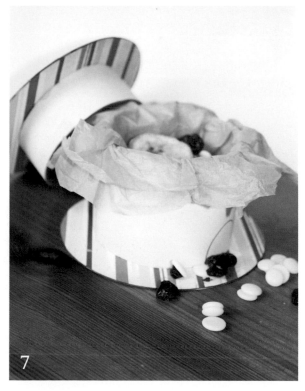

Origami Star Gift Box

There are websites dedicated to origami and once you try this star gift box you will be hooked. Who knew that folding paper could become so addictive?

You will need your basic equipment plus:
- 20x20cm piece of patterned paper
- Decorations and embellishments

Step Two. Fold in half again.

Step Three. Bring over the left-hand flap over and press flat. This is called a squash fold.

Step One. Start by making a basic origami square. You will need to fold the paper in half.

Step Four. Flip the paper over.

Step Five. Repeat the squash fold for the final flap.

Step Six. You now have your basic square.

Step Seven. Fold the right side up to the centre crease.

Step Eight. Open up this new fold and flatten, press firmly to strengthen the crease.

Step Nine. Repeat steps 2 and 3 for the left-hand side.

Step Ten. Turn over the paper and repeat all of the steps so you have identical points on both sides of your box.

Step Eleven. Bring the top flap over and press firmly.

Step Twelve. Fold both sides in to meet centre crease.

Step Thirteen. Turn and repeat.

Step Fourteen. Fold the point so that it lays over the top of the box.

Step Fifteen. Repeat for the other 3 sides.

Step Sixteen. Gently pull at the points while pressing the base flat on a table, the box will open ready for use.

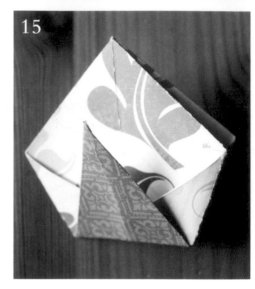

Suitcase Gift Box

Packaging for men's gifts is extremely hard – sometimes harder than buying the gift in the first place! Socks anyone? With this fabulous little suitcase, you can package handmade treats for the man in your life and never be short of gifts in the future.

You will need your basic equipment plus:
- 21x28cm piece of cardstock
- Scissors
- Double-sided tape
- Crafters Companion Score Board (available from stockist listed on page 192)
- Scoring tool
- Decorations and embellishments

Step One. You need to start with a 8.5x11cm piece of cardstock (either patterned or plain depending on if you want to decorate when you are finished). Fold in half and score to create a fold down the middle of the page.

Step Two. If you are using the Ultimate score board, you need to line your centre fold up with the 13cm square fold mark and score at both lines either side. If you are working with a scoring tool and ruler you need to measure and score at 2.5cm either side of your initial score line.

Step Three. With an Ultimate score board, move your initial fold up to the half fold A4 line and then score down the gatefold A5 line. With a scoring tool and ruler, measure and score at 7.5cm and 10cm marks from the last score line you made. Turn your cardstock and do the same for the other side, making both sides of your initial score line identical.

Step Four. Move this score line to the gatefold A4 mark and score again down the gatefold A5 line. Turn and do the same for the other side, making both sides identical.

Step Five. Turn your paper portrait and score down the gatefold A5 line at both sides. Or score 5.5cm in from either side.

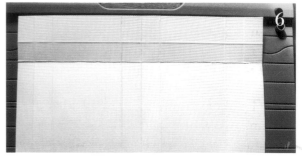

Step Six. Score now at 2.5cm from that line and 2.5cm again, leaving a .5cm margin to be trimmed off. Or from the 5.5cm line, make 2 more score lines at 2.5cm each, leaving a 5mm margin to be trimmed off.

Step Seven. Fold and score all of these lines to give them a sharp finish. Trim off the pieces as shown.

Step Eight. Place double-sided tape on all of the bits to be folded in and over.

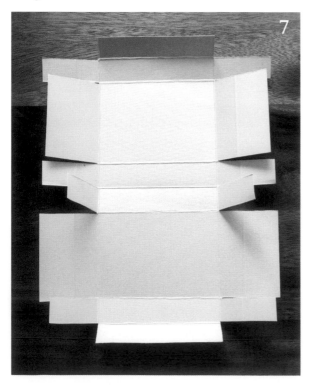

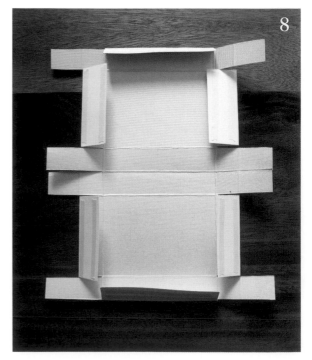

Step Nine. Do one half of the box at a time. Fold the side reinforcements in on the sides and bring the outer side pieces up and over. Do the same for the front.

Step Ten. Do the same for the top section and you should have what resembles a little open suitcase.

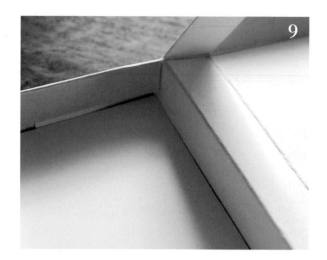

Step Eleven. To make the barrier for inside, cut a strip of sturdy card 25cm long. Score at 7.5cm from both edges. Place inside the box and trim if necessary.

Step Twelve. Once you are happy with the fit, you can scallop the edge (I used scissors to run around the edge). Fasten into the box with double-sided tape.

Step Thirteen. Make sure your box closes securely. The lid will stay shut with just the insert keeping it in place. Decorate with ribbons, lace, buttons and bows.

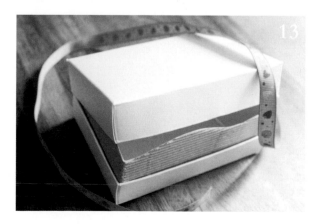

Where to Buy

A Trip Down Memory Lane
Patterned paper, cardstock, double-sided tape,
embellishments
www.atripdownmemorylane.co.uk
01787 210 272

City Attic
Cake stands, decorative plates, home décor,
presentation ideas
www.cityattic.co.uk
0191 370 9802

Crafters Companion
Trimmers, box making boards, cardstock, rubber
stamps
www.crafterscompanion.co.uk
0845 296 0042

Crafty Ribbons
Ribbons, buttons and bows
www.craftyribbons.com
01258 455889

Hobbycraft
Craft papers, candy melts, lolly sticks, patterned
paper, cardstock.
www.hobbycraft.co.uk
0845 051 6547

Just a Soap
All ingredients for making soap and other natural
cosmetics
www.justasoap.co.uk
01842 855975

Lakeland
Baking supplies, cake decoration, preserving
bottles and jars
www.lakeland.co.uk
01539 488 100

Make a Wish Cake Shop
Edible gold leaf, cake decoration, cake decorating
equipment, baking tins
www.makeawishcakeshop.co.uk

Papertrey Ink
Stamps, paper, ink, ribbons, tools and boxes
www.papertreyink.com

Typhoon
Kitchen scales, oil bottles, kitchenware
www.typhoonhousewares.com
0151 486 1888

UKScrappers
Crafting inspiration from around the world.
www.ukscrappers.co.uk